Is It Enough To Be Nice?

for everyone

Is It Enough To Be Nice?

David Jackman

Second edition © David Jackman 2024
www.david-jackman.co.uk
Set in PSFournier 12/14pt
Design by Sarah Jackman

Previously issued as *Ou-Boum: In Search of a Kinder Society?*

Ou-Boum is the central expression in E. M. Forster's *A Passage to India* (1924) used to describe the haunting echo of the Marabar caves – Boum, the utter emptiness of nothingness, while Ou, respecting the Hindu or Buddhist 'Om', suggests the wholeness and goodness of everything…

Passages from Forster's work used throughout with the kind permission of The Provost and Scholars of King's College, Cambridge and the Society of Authors.

ISBN 978 1 73933 980 7

Table of Contents

About the Author	i
Acknowledgements	iii
A Note on TTP	iii
Foreword	iv

Part A: What?

1	The Endgame	3
2	Heavy Salad	7
3	Only Connect	16
	Map	23

Part B: How?

4	Place	31
5	Principle	35
6	People	46
	Charter	68

Part C: Why?

7	Crossing the Stream	77
8	Mysteries	83
9	The Power of the Dog	87
10	Coming Home	91

Conclusion	99
Epilogue	101

About the Author

Maybe an only child just wants everyone to be kind? But then, is it enough to be 'nice'?

School was dull, but after Oxford (studying, in part, ethics), and a long summer in India, I started on a high-level banking career in The City. On the bus home I took to reading *A Passage to India*, rekindling memories of warm, still Delhi mornings, and firing a fascination with the spaces through which we travel. Forster's expression *Ou-Boum* piercing the tension between self and other, reverberates throughout this book. We follow E. M. Forster's structure of three formative spaces; the intellectual, physical and spiritual - and find what lies beyond.

During a brief excursion into teaching, via Cambridge, I discovered methodologies for using these ideas about formative spaces in a way that I was in a position to apply, as a senior regulator, across the full sweep of financial regulation, including being the first regulator to introduce a focus on ethics, culture and corporate maturity. These are now mainstream.

Having also previously established a professional institute, led an industry skills council and set up a university business initiative, we 'cut across country' to the Lake District, and the home of Wordsworth (who we often reference), to develop a portfolio of non-executive directorships, consultancies and professional education. Staying ahead of the curve, I led and authored many UK and international (ISO) standards for sustainability, corporate social responsibility, sustainable cities and communities (ISO 37101 series) and now co-chair the ISO committee on ESG (Environmental, Social and Governance).

This book, provoked by serious illness (TTP) and completed under lockdown, aims to make sense of a lifetime's body of work, much of which seemed disconnected at the time, and to take ideas forward into the personal realm and apply them to whole communities. Each chapter contains a piece of the jigsaw, scattered with autobiographical fragments to provide some colour and context. And finally, we seek to answer, like Forster, whether there is 'anything on earth, or in the heavens above...worth writing about'.[1]

Two earlier volumes on collective corporate maturity:
The Compliance Revolution, Wiley, Singapore, 2015
Corporate Maturity and the Authentic Company, BEP, New York, 2018

---

[1] J.M. Murray, 1924, quoted in the introduction to the 1978 Penguin edition of *A Passage to India*.

Acknowledgements

Heartfelt thanks to Dr Dutt and the staff of the Royal Liverpool University Hospital who quite literally saved my life; and my wife and family for all their love and support.

Special thanks to Rev. Canon Cameron Butland for his help on The Charter and Chapter 8, and to our daughter, Sarah, for her help on design and for inspiring the Conclusion, the first section to be written. Thanks too for Mo's inspiration, the contribution of many Grasmere societies, Alexander's proofreading and Dr Will Smith's assistance with publication.

A note on TTP

татьян TTP (Thrombotic Thrombocytopenic Purpura) is a rare and life-threatening auto-immune blood disorder. Micro blood clots form throughout the body when a crucial anti-clotting protein called Adamts13 is inhibited by an over-active immune system. Failure to treat the condition leads to multiple organ failure.

Treatment consists of plasma exchange followed by immunotherapy and relapse is common. There are a few specialist centres, one fortunately in Liverpool. Greater recognition of TTP would be helpful so cases can be referred rapidly.

Foreword

A Present for Matty

I remember trying to get our younger son to sleep when he was about three, quietly composing what a child might understand as a simple view of humanity:

We are one family, with one home,
and we share a common life.

We all have the same needs and wants, hopes and fears.

We can all help each other;
to find 'good,'
to love and be loved,
and to belong.

Our son is now much older and in work, but this early formulation offers us a starting point. Now we need an altogether more substantive discussion.

David Jackman
Easedale
The Lake District
2nd April 2023

Part A: What?

Chapter 1
The Endgame

'Nothing will come of nothing.'
William Shakespeare, *King Lear*, Act 1, Scene 1[1]

Tragedy is only a step away. Lying in intensive care on a crowded Friday night in Liverpool, there was a chance to reflect. A just-in-time diagnosis of TTP (Thrombotic Thrombocytopenic Purpura), a rare auto-immune blood clotting disorder, saved my life. Christmas was spent with a plasma exchange line in my neck.

We don't prepare ourselves for death. Better not to talk about it... but its proximity prompts re-evaluation. Some moments in life stand out as being worthwhile, but much recedes into greyness. When we - or others - come to weigh our lives, we usually give the greatest value to how we have treated others, our closest relationships, the good we might have done and our contribution to the community.

Nobody recites a curriculum vitae in a eulogy.

---

[1] From the opening scene of Shakespeare's *King Lear*, our favourite play, and recalling the RSC's performance at the Theatre Royal, Newcastle in 2007 with Sir Ian McKellan.

No one remembers what you had. We all know, instinctively, that none of that really counts. However, we do acknowledge the aspects of our lives that feel important. A fundamental mystery is why we spend so much time and energy on what we recognise is not particularly worthwhile and so little time on what we know, deep down, matters?

A Necessary Journey

We learn as we go along to address this basic question and get better at striking a sensible balance, but often it is very difficult, and we realise our miscalculations too late. This is both distressing and frustrating – think of the good we could have done!

This book is about how we might be better able to find a more positive way forward earlier on, before it seems too late. In fact, getting this balance is part of expressing and fulfilling our essential humanity – what it means to be human. This struggle to find a more human way of doing things is central to discovering who we are, being the best we can be and navigating between self and other.

We will find that we are forever learning, testing and trying out new ways to strike this balance and to develop a more resilient approach to life. This life-long journey is a form of growing-up and, in particular, of maturing our core humanity. The centrality of this task makes this 'the necessary journey'.

This necessary journey of maturing our humanity will not usually move forward very smoothly or effectively on its own, but needs some specific and conscious effort to progress. The purpose of this book is to explicitly focus on this central and pivotal challenge (accepting that we face many other important challenges, the success of which may well hinge upon the success of the core journey) and to provide a series of tools, maps and ideas to help us on our way.

A Collective Journey

We also recognise that this is not a journey we make alone, but we travel together and mature collectively, as well as individually. Later we will demonstrate how we need to help each other if we are going to mature at all - it is necessarily a collective journey.

Furthermore, if, for whatever reason, any one of us does not (or cannot) mature it affects us all and we will find it more difficult to mature both individually and collectively.

Finally, a warning: prevarication and perfectionism are two comfort blankets that we cannot afford. How often do we say 'I'll just finish this... and then I'll have time to ...'? Except the list of jobs never ends, and we never find time to reflect or change... Failing to engage in this core, necessary journey is the real tragedy. If we let this journey pass us by, we will be 'borne back'[2] by the tide and risk ending up where we began, as Lear warns, with nothing.

Contents of the book

It is always harder to be clear than complicated. We will attempt to be brief and straightforward, accessible and

---

[2] F. Scott Fitzgerald, *The Great Gatsby*, 1925 'So we beat on, boats against the current, borne back ceaselessly into the past.'

practical, with only the barest of references. But this is not to say we aim to be simplistic. It is recognised throughout that we are dealing with issues that are inherently both complex and profound.

Part A seeks to identify what matters most and what constitutes the core of our humanity. We set out on our collective journey of maturing humanity. A Map is offered to guide us.

Part B provides tools to help us on our journey and suggests measures of maturity. There is also a Charter.

Part C asks the difficult questions about 'why mature?' and what is the significance of our journey and suggests where we end up.

The Epilogue draws these threads together.

Chapter 2
Heavy Salad

'We have learned nothing from history
People are dead in their lifetimes ...
Systems are huge
The traffic keeps moving, proving there's nothing to do
It's a big business baby, and its smile is hideous
Top-down violence, a structural viciousness'
    Kae Tempest, *Let Them Eat Chaos*, 2016

Early Questions

I clearly remember asking myself, aged 5, 'Why do we make things worse? To be more precise, 'Why do we do what we don't want to do and not what we want to do?' I know where I was at the time - standing beside my mother after school on the village green. I can see it now, my mother, who underneath it all was the kindest and most caring of people, having a conversation with another mother who was being really unpleasant and, I thought, unnecessarily competitive. Why behave like this? Maybe an only child just wants everyone to be 'nice'.

Two questions have driven much of my thinking and practice since then:

(a) Why do we not do what we want to do?

(b) Why do we so often make maturity harder for ourselves and others?

Systems

Some would say the economic and social systems fail because of inherent human weakness, endemic incompetence, and lazy negligence. The many apparent human shortcomings are compounded by an internalised fatalism. We are told... or we imagine ... that being nice is somehow 'soft.' Kindness will undoubtedly be taken advantage of on occasion, but does that risk mean that we all need to live out our whole lives cautiously, defensively and selfishly?

Perhaps we have bought into a narrative that as humans are fundamentally flawed, we are unworthy of a better life. We may, therefore, give up early or 'squander [our] resistance, for a pocketful of mumbles, such are promises'[1] ... Disenchantment can lead to a self-centred approach of taking what you can and letting 'the devil take the hindmost'. We can seek substitutes for satisfaction but nothing can compensate for knowing we are accepting second-best. Certainly, markets commoditise and corrupt relationships, but if we were to have better ideas is it feasible for anyone to stand up to the pressure of what we see as the system? Anyway, for many like Oliver Stone's Gordon Gekko, 'greed is good' and 'justice, like lunch, is for wimps.'[2]

---

[1] From Simon and Garfunkel, *The Boxer*, 1969
[2] Oliver Stone, *Wall Street*, 1987

Adam Smith[3] claimed that running an economy on good intentions is simply too unreliable and only an economy depending on the base instincts of self-interest and competition could be sufficiently predictable and efficient. Darwin's evolutionary theories rely on similar mechanisms and have become translated into the way we view societies.[4] Smith did believe that 'social goods' would spin-off and trickle down to the benefit of all, as if by an 'invisible hand'. But experience has shown that unrestrained competitive systems tend to concentrate wealth rather than distribute these goods. The viable opportunities to make different choices and live according to your own values are severely restricted.

These dilemmas reflect an age-old debate. William Morris' *News from Nowhere* saw that:

> industrial capitalism ... has alienated the human working agent not only from the products of his or her labour, but also from what is natural – from what is natural for human beings and from the world of concrete sensation that is the basis of how we make serious and lasting meanings for ourselves, believing life only has value when you attribute value to the lives of others.[5]

Similarly, John Ruskin, living in Brantwood, in nearby Coniston, sought to demonstrate how craftsmanship exhibits 'the lamp of sacrifice' - the willingness to

---

[3]   Adam Smith, *The Wealth of Nations*, 1776
[4]   Charles Darwin, *On the Origin of Species*, 1859
[5]   William Morris, *News from Nowhere*, 1890, discovered at Blackwell

do something well for its own sake and for others.' ⁶ Ruskin's simple conclusion is relevant today - 'There is no wealth but life.'

William Wordsworth, living in Grasmere in the early part of the 19th century and one of the forerunners of the environmental and National Park movements, bemoaned in *The Recluse* what 'man has made of man' ... he lamented:

> [Man]... truly is alone,
> He of the multitude whose eyes are doomed
> To hold a vacant commerce day by day
> With objects wanting life-repelling love; ...
> Where numbers overwhelm humanity
> And neighbourhood serves rather to divide
> Than to unite.

In his pastoral poem 'Michael', Wordsworth saw the tearing of the fundamental connections between people and the land as the root cause of much dislocation. It was his own closeness to nature that caused him to ponder, often in this very valley: 'On man, the heart of man, and human life'.⁷

Canon Hardwicke Rawnsley and his wife Edith, living at Allan Bank further along the same valley in Grasmere a few decades later, focused on practical solutions - such as the Keswick School of Industrial Art - and Hardwicke was a co-founder of the National Trust. However, such idealised romantic visions became, as so

---

⁶   John Ruskin, *The Seven Lamps of Architecture*, 1901

⁷   William Wordsworth, 'Michael: A Pastoral Poem', *Lyrical Ballads*, 1800

often is the case, an indulgence of an affluent few.

So, we must be careful not to continue an appalling condescension. For the Dhaka textile worker or the Delhi rickshaw-wallah[8] concepts of a 'better life' must seem a risible, first-world self-indulgence. Even driving down Walton Road back from The Royal Hospital in Liverpool, passing a rotation of tattoo parlours, vape shops, bookies, takeaways, and shuttered empty buildings – lifestyle choices must seem as a 'foreign country.' While we know that the poorest in our communities are often the warmest and most generous, the only kindness or respite they may receive comes at life's end, back in The Royal. No one should romanticise their situation or judge the choices they make. But we also know that being relatively wealthy doesn't guarantee maturity or wisdom either. Being our better selves rarely is a matter of money.

Individualism

One obstacle to striking a balance between self and other is the growing eulogisation of self-worth and individualism. 'Be yourself', 'do anything you want to do', 'me, me, me!'.... This sometimes-exhausting sense of entitlement, self-expression and identity can shade into victimhood and confected outrage. But 'Just do it' ... 'Because I'm worth it' represents forms of self-referencing value that is almost free of any external perspective. Self-indulgence can become even more narcissistic in

---

[8] Vishwas, 'All for Rs 10K or Less a Month' *Citizen Matters*, June 16, 2019. http://citizenmatters.in/noida-migrant-rickshaw-pullers-wages-rentals-living-conditions-13046

a virtual, algorithmic and infantilising social media world, flattened by disinterest and disconnection. This disjuncture is likely to disengage anyone from any sense of a collective journey – undermined further by a moral superiority or self-righteousness that disdains real responsibility and seeks to oppress, divide and push others away. We would do well to take breath and remind ourselves regularly 'it's not all about me'.

Self-absorption seems to stand in stark contrast to the apparent selflessness and self-sacrifice of our parents' generation. They took, arguably, too much trouble and were too ready to be sacrificial. I recall every school trip my Mother would make a packed lunch of marmite and cucumber sandwiches carefully wrapped in greaseproof with a thin brown elastic band. School green cardigans were always buttoned up ... "keep warm, and careful how you cross the road!" However it could also be that expressions of gentle kindness revealed another form of moral superiority, often based on education, and reinforced by craving self-deprecation and oh-so-worthy deferred enjoyment.

The Human Condition

How do we resolve the internal tensions within each of us and between self and selflessness? Maslow proposed a hierarchy of needs that suggested we satisfy basic needs first - such as shelter, warmth, and food – before devoting more time to higher-order needs such as love and what he called 'self-actualisation'.[9] But this implied delay in higher fulfilment brings with it the implication

---

[9]   Abraham Maslow, *A Theory of Human Motivation in Psychological Review*, 1943

of significant collateral damage and lost opportunity that bakes in an acerbic attitude to life with attendant stress and poor mental health.

How do we make things worse?

Pursuing a primarily selfish course makes it harder for others to be selfless and to 'correct our course' later, because, in Maslow's terms:

1. If we use up most of our time and effort on self-centred needs then, simply put, we will have run out of resources and road for anything we might see as more worthwhile.

2. If we always try to have our cake and eat it, in other words suppose that selfish aims can also operate for the general good (the so-called win: win or middle-way options), usually we end up with second-rate compromises that fail by both yardsticks.

3. Kidding ourselves by fudging the distinction between self and other erodes discernment and integrity, the ability to differentiate at all between the interests of self and others.

4. If we do achieve some higher order aims, we may be tempted to 'bank' what we have, while pulling up the ladder so that others behind cannot follow.[10]

---

[10] St John Climacus (550-649), Abbot of Mount Sinai, at the top rung of his *Ladder of Heavenly Ascent*. A late 12th century icon.

5. By perpetuating the belief in the primacy of competition we inherently feed a system that cannot reverse or afford to repay our trust, nor ever be forgiving or redemptive.

There will be many other reasons too.

Maturity

Maybe we also need to say to ourselves – "just grow up!" If we start by assuming that almost all humans have roughly similar over-riding aims and values, why should it be so hard to work together to achieve these common goals that benefit everyone?
    Simply put, even in a small way (whatever our circumstances and condition), we can choose to make different choices ...

1. We need to learn how to strike a better balance between self and selfless interests as we mature our humanity – and help others to do the same.

2. We need to mature in a way that does not make it more difficult for others to follow.

    In helping ourselves and others to mature we must be wary of simplistic formulae. There has been a focus on 'quick fixes' giving rise to concepts of quality of life, mindfulness, self-discovery, wellbeing, or self-fulfilment. All useful but often representing more of the same - different versions of self.
    Finding a way forward is inherently difficult and complicated. There will be plenty of failure, confusion and discomfort. Maturity requires the grittiness of a

5-day test match cricket, more than the dash of a T20 game. Maturity is inherently hard work – but worth it.

Maturity, as Terry my new friend from Liverpool concludes, is *heavy salad*.

Chapter 3
Only Connect

'Only connect! ...'

'...That was the whole of her sermon. Only connect the prose and the passion, and both will be exalted, and human love will be seen at its height. Live in fragments no longer. Only connect, and the beast and the monk, robbed of the isolation that is life to either, will die.'

E.M. Forster, *Howard's End*, 1910

We might connect with places or people or principles, for example. Paradoxically, in an age of unparalleled connectivity, we can seem more distant, disengaged, and disconnected than ever. How is it that a moment when I felt profoundly connected to all three, I was alone, in a desolate chapel in Little Town, beneath Hindscarth in the Newlands Valley, just over Greenup Edge?

What to connect with?

If we are to find a better balance between self and other, we need to be more aware of the 'other' we are connecting with. Taking the three core human needs identified in the Foreword – all forms of connection with 'other' - as a reasonable starting point:

1) to belong
2) finding good
3) to love and be loved

...we can explore what each might look like in practice.

To belong

We can connect with the structures, spaces and places that hold our lives together – home, family, friends, our land, community, region, country and ultimately the world family. Our connection may be through a tapestry of art, music, language, laws, faiths, industries and sports. All of these structures and practices are expressed and embedded in landscapes and cultures which ensures their continuance and facilitates their evolution. An inheritance handed down from one generation to the next, through images, traditions and narratives of shared experiences, holding collectively in trust the good and bad for those who follow on. We continue to enjoy the richness of our heritage through celebrations and creativity. We are inspired to explore new places, discovering and adventuring, while creating new wealth and nurturing sustainable lives and the environment. This includes sharing the visceral cycle of birth, life and death, the diurnal round, the seasons, and patterns of life that together form what we may call creation. We can lose ourselves in belonging to the whole that is beyond ourselves.

Finding good

Our common principles, values and ethics are shared conceptions of what might be considered 'good' or 'right', giving common priorities and morals. Refined by nuances that help us to make fine judgments on tough decisions and allow us to say no when necessary. Empowering others and ourselves to create enough space to grow and to make judgments by balancing differing interests. Committing to 'good' in a self-less way without seeking return or reward. Challenging self-interest, privilege and entitlement and shining a light into dark corners. Overcoming obfuscation and bureaucracy, being transparent and accountable even under pressure. Showing leadership and wisdom and being brave where necessary. Building hope and faith, dealing with failure and mistakes, and allowing for forgiveness and redemption.

To love and be loved

Helping and caring for others, giving to others freely. Finding common cause and interests based on mutuality, fair exchange, shared heritage, common experiences and ties of association and kinship. The longer we spend together with other people usually the greater the sense of continuity and understanding of each other's strengths and failings and our respective roles and contributions. Ensuring everyone is included and valued, while celebrating diversity. Dignity comes from being able to make a contribution to the whole and the deep satisfaction that this contribution, however slight, is recognised and valued by the community. Depending on others, as others depend on us. Sharing responsibility builds up our common life. Helping each other with gentle humour and common kindness.

Maturity of humanity

These three threads are suggested as the core of being human. These three are based on lifetime of observation, research and reading and self-reflection. Of course, other dimensions could be included. For example, creativity and freedom are fundamental dimensions of humanity. Both are hugely important to our essential humanity, but creativity and the natural tendency to grow and develop, has been incorporated in the general heading of belonging, while at least some degree of freedom is a prerequisite for all three to flourish. In fact, it would not matter if other elements were included so long as they were followed through the entire model that follows. It is hoped that dimensions are as general and inclusive as possible.

In any case, these three threads are closely interrelated and become increasingly inter-twinned with time and maturity.... The process of developing closer and deeper connections we see as maturity, or the maturing of the core of our common humanity.

How to connect

How do we make these valuable connections, and how do we deepen and mature them?

We will find that forming and maturing these critical bonds depends to a degree on giving and receiving. We are not necessarily talking about one-for-one transactions, giving *x* for *y* in return, but more of an open state in which we are willing to offer something of ourselves (usually not money) while also receiving some of the good that surrounds us.

We will see in the Map that follows that as we

give and receive more, our connections deepen and mature. We identify four distinct Stages of maturity to create a General Model of Maturing our Humanity. In Part B we will see how this deepening of connections can be facilitated and in Part C we see how maturity changes us, and more importantly, how we end up in quite a different place.

Postscript

This pattern of intertwining routes is wonderfully represented in Bryan Winter's series of paintings of *Galician Streams* at the Tate Gallery in St Ives.[1] His notes say:

> A stream finds its way over rocks. The force of the stream and the quality of the rocks determine the stream's bed. This in turn modifies the course of the stream, channelling out new sluices and hollows. The stream erodes the rock, the rock deflects the stream, until, at some high point, the stream bursts its banks and falls into a ravine. The dry streambed, carved and hollowed, remains. Its form contains its history.

---

[1] The estate of Bryan Wynter, Tate, St Ives

Indicators of Maturity of our Humanity

Characteristics of maturity could include:

1. A gentle sense of humour, self-deprecating and sensitive, simple common kindness. Generosity of grace and self-giving. Compassionate.

2. Still, settled, peaceful, collected and calm; with space to reflect and contemplate and see more deeply.

3. Delight in the energy of life, new mornings, new life, growth, maturity and achievement; marked by a thankfulness for the warmth of fellowship and freedom.

4. Vital, imaginative and free-thinking. Creating beauty. Nuanced sophistication, a richness of design and elegance, artistry and craftsmanship.

5. Enjoying the wonder, marvel and awe of life. Fostering wild imagination and discovery, thinking for ourselves, sharing our knowledge and experience, being brave, sticking out our necks and taking (reasonable) risks. Being unashamedly unusual. Being all right with not knowing and uncertainty. Free to be wrong.

6. Tolerant and celebrating difference and challenge, not-rushing to judgement, finding maturity. Overcoming fears and prejudices.

7. Trying hard, but accepting failures and then happily learning and taking responsibility and accountability. Open and cooperative. Never obscuring or obfuscating. Believing in a second chance. Showing leadership where we can.

8.   Responsible, having integrity. Seeking fairness and justice, not asking for favour or preference or privilege or entitlement. Loyal, resilient, and reliable. Respectful and supporting dignity.

9.   Valuing life in all its fullness and in its muddled messiness – the visceral and gritty and grounded – helping each other with the inevitable illness, hurt, debilitation, confusion, defeat, damage, disorder, distress, despair, death and tragedy.

10.   Strong, defending values and the good that bind us together. Putting ourselves out for others. Seeking wisdom or discernment to make good choices. Authentic and genuine. Looking beyond. Hopeful and redemptive.

Map

'Life is half spent, before we know what it is.'
George Herbert, *Jacula Prudentum*, 1651

Before we travel it is useful to have a map. As a dyed-in-the-wool, 'regional' geographer (and orienteer), I would say a proper map is one that sets out the whole context and allows your eyes to wander around and enjoy the landscape. Maps give insights into a bigger picture[1] and provide a much-needed bridge between theory and practice. Maps also give a sense of direction, allow an evaluation of progress as well as direct us towards our possible next steps and help to assess different options and routes.

This General Model of Maturing our Humanity builds on a similar model of corporate maturity, first published in 2002 as a regulator and revised and re-published in 2015 and 2018.

---

[1]   Inspired by David Hockney's exhibition of the same name at the Royal Academy in 2012 and school mate Grayson Perry's *Red Carpet* 2017.

General Model of Maturing our Humanity

Stages   Social and community indicators

4 Values-led   Internalised principles, acting responsibly because we want to, not obligation. Fairness and ethical principles at the heart of society and economic outcomes. Able to place others' interests ahead of our own. Capable of answering 'why?'. Making fine ethical distinctions, handling uncomfortable tensions. Not rule-bound. Seeking 'spirit' not letter. Whole greater than sum of parts. Emphasis on co-operation, freedom, mutuality and common cause and vision. Conscious building of human maturity. Connected to place, principle, people. Space for empowerment, creativity, innovation, education and capacity. Spiritual, artistic dimensions part of rounded measures. Authenticity, genuineness and integrity. Diversity, equality and integration. Sustainability / ESG stewardship key. Confidence in values, duties and role. Caring for weak and less fortunate. Fun, humour and common kindness.

3 Commitment Looking for efficiencies and win: wins, but ultimately self-interested. Opportunistic and reactive. Siloed and dislocation / disengagement. Growing confidence, adaptability, willingness to be inventive, creative risks. Growing empowerment and learning culture. Individual responsibility and sense of ownership. Accountability and constructive challenge embedded in culture of common sense and good governance. Acceptance of mistakes. Engrossed in screen-life. Reliance on good process over-rides good outcome.

Stages	Social and community indicators
2 Compliance	Bound by external standards and values, unthinking bureaucratic and mechanistic decision-making by the letter; culture of dependency / entitlement. Heavily regulated. Comfort-blanket of regulation - outsourcing or 'laundering of conscience'. Limited personal accountability, weasel words, obfuscation. Mediocre standards. Following not leading. Conservative socially, maybe intolerant, often divided, with inequalities.
1 Minimum standards	Focus on simplistic over-arching aims e.g. economic growth. Abdicates / diffuses responsibility and accountability. Enforcement fear. Inequality. Limited protections and human rights. Limited transparency and opportunities - especially for vulnerable groups. Little investment in education or long-term vision. Risk of abuse / corruption / violence / war.

The model should be read from the bottom

Four similar Stages are identified:

1. Minimum standards – primarily self-interested

2. Compliance – connecting but in a bureaucratic way. A lack of understanding of values and vision. Inability to be selective and make judgements. External standards are applied by prescriptive rules.

3. Commitment – deepening connections, forming more reliable relationships but still partly conditional.

4. Values-led – Internalised values (because you want to rather than because you have to) with humanity at their core.

The model can be viewed at three scales:

1. Long-term trajectory of the whole of humanity
2. Societies or communities
3. Individual

The map offers indicators of individual or community maturity for each of the four Stages.

Maturity is rarely linear or smooth, and often stalls or declines for a while. The model is a generalisation and is designed to provide an overall view. Part B provides more detail on the Stages and how maturity could be facilitated.

Maturity is a product of the human tendency to learn and grow. The Model is built from many others' development models such as those from educational development, including Piaget's model of cognitive development.[2] The Model does not cover

---

[2] See Jean Piaget, *The Moral Judgment of the Child*, London, Routledge & Kegan Paul, 1932. Lawrence Kohlberg, 'Stage and Sequence: The Cognitive-Developmental Approach to Socialization' in *Handbook of Socialization Theory and Research*, ed. D.A. Goslin, Chicago, Rand McNally, 1969. Lawrence Kohlberg, *Essays on Moral Development Volume 1: The Philosophy of Moral Development*, San Francisco, Harper & Row, 1981.

all aspects of human development, such as economic growth, technological progress, social maturity, artistic 'civilisation' and intellectual development, but rather focuses on the values and ethics at the heart of humanity. Of course, there are connections between all of these aspects and parallels could be drawn.

The far horizon of the Model potentially shifts ever upward through history, and we cannot say where this may move in the future. But the map allows us to evaluate our relative position and guide us toward the next steps that are visible now. Finally, as we connect more deeply, we change and so we may conclude that in some small way the wider whole also changes and matures with us.

Other maps

Parallel models have been published by the author for businesses and organisations, and for regulators.[3] These, in particular, highlight the difficulties that come from a short-sighted strategy of trying to avoid maturing by 'outsourcing conscience' and relying on box-ticking and regulation.[4] These models show that simply having good processes does not necessarily result in good outcomes.

---

[3] See the author's *The Compliance Revolution*, Singapore, Wiley 2015 and *Ethics for Regulators* for the Parliamentary Committee on Standards in Public Life
[4] David Jackman, 'Business won't be ethical until it shares society's values again,' *The Independent*, 12 July 2012. https://www.independent.co.uk/voices/commentators/david-jackman-business-won-t-be-ethical-until-it-shares-society-s-values-again-7965044.html

Part B: How?

Here we focus on the core connections and tools that help us on our journey.

Chapter 4
Place

'... We all need space. Unless we have it, we cannot reach that sense of quiet in which whispers of better things come to us gently.'
Octavia Hill, 1883 Co-founder of the National Trust

My father passed on one piece of advice from his long experience in education when I started teaching - 'make [the pupils] do the work'. Creating spaces in which people are encouraged to engage and grapple with complex concepts helps learning and effective decision-making. It is important not to offer answers too soon, but to create a safe place where everyone can explore, question, and form their own views. These spaces encourage us to own, be accountable for, and carry through these decisions.

Place and space

How can we help ourselves and others make connections? Place provides one context and a framework for developing maturity. Place shapes our common life by embedding the structures, patterns, processes and systems and effectively passes these on to successive generations. Living and working together we build an interdependence through mutual interests.

A simple question we may ask ourselves about place is where is 'home'? This can be a complicated question. Is it where we were born (in my case, Hertfordshire, a place I can hardly remember), or where our parents and family came from (largely Devon), or where we have our happiest years (Chilterns), or spent the longest time (Essex, to which I feel little connection at all)) or worked (London) ... or just where we now live and have 'hefted' (the Lake District)? Do we connect more with places where we took significant decisions or steps: Alnmouth and Selva (first outdoor jobs), Lavenham (where we were married), Singapore (where I have travelled over 50 times) or Delhi (on my first visit to India)? Or is there a connection that comes down the ages? We can say that for generations our family has one place close to all our hearts, White Hart Lane (now the Tottenham Hotspur Stadium). Whatever the motivation, a palimpsest of significant places becomes the framework in which we formulate and re-formulate our 'home'.

Space is a form of abstracted place i.e., without specific location. We can deliberately create spaces to facilitate almost anywhere as structures that will enable maturity. Creating spaces, either consciously or incidentally, or as a by-product of some other endeavour, plays an important part in fostering the maturing of our humanity.

Creating Crucibles

Spaces – that can be both real or virtual - can act as a 'crucible' holding many elements together, possibly under tension or pressure, allowing something new and valuable, greater than the sum of the parts, to be forged. For example, crucibles create a decision-making environment where difficult issues and questions can be raised and hopefully resolved.

Obviously, crucibles are not meant to be perfectly controlled environments and part of the learning process is to expect unexpected results. A crucible is a forum for generating a more structured and purposeful discussion but they will not necessarily produce a 'correct' or even a straightforward 'answer.'

Spaces can be created to facilitate our journey, whether in work, through policy formation and regulation, in society or government, at home or in our communities. However, the greater the amount of discussion, bringing in diverse and sometimes conflicting views, the more likely it is that we will produce more rounded, mature and human decisions.

Components of a Crucible

Vision, direction and standards

Cultures, traditions and landscapes

Governance, structures, organisations, responsibilities

Values and ethics

1.	Creating strong boundaries – the walls of the crucible need to be robust principles and are constructed of solid and secure blocks of familiar practice or experience. The lid provides direction, such as collective vision, direction and standards, while values and ethics offer a solid base. Careful control or good governance makes sure that the mistakes that will inevitably occur are not too damaging to the whole.
2.	The space within the crucible allows for open discussion, reflection and insight ... and sufficient empowerment to make and own decisions that participants can then own and be accountable for. Mistakes will be made but can be managed in a way that recognises them as essential for learning.
3.	Maturity may require an existing prescription to be relaxed over time in a careful and planned way so that pre-determined right answers can be phased out, or become not so readily available. Without removing rote answers and box-ticking no one will mature very far or gain the associated sense of responsibility.

Crucibles can be anywhere, a theatre, a business meeting, an open community session, a family dining table, a sports match or a place of worship. Crucibles are not designed to deliver pre-cooked solutions but facilitate an open debate for all, empowering everyone in everyday situations to be involved and invested in decisions. They offer quite literally 'room to deny ourselves.'[1] The spaces offer the opportunity of a collective discipline such as Constructive Challenge as we shall see in the next Chapter.

---

[1] John Keble, *New Every Morning is the Love*, 1822

Chapter 5
Principle

'My whole life, I secretly very much wanted two paintings made ... My own portrait and... A picture of bliss ... In actuality, we don't look for smiles in pictures of bliss, but rather, for the happiness in life itself. Painters know this, but this is precisely what they cannot depict. That's why they substitute the joy of seeing for the joy of life.'
Orhan Pamuk, *My Name is Red*, 1998

I made my first and, at that time, ground-breaking speech as a regulator on ethics and culture at the Drapers' Hall in Throgmorton Street in the City of London almost exactly 20 years ago on Halloween, 2002. It was revolutionary at the time – the first regulator to set out an ethical framework for financial services. The ethics cited for organisations (and drawn from statute) were...

- *Open, honest, responsive, and accountable*
- *Committed to acting competently, responsibly, and reliably*
- *Relating to colleagues and customers fairly and with respect*

These kinds of principles are now accepted as mainstream and have become key to financial regulation internationally. Ethics are not the answer to everything, but they do contribute an important perspective to constructive challenge, decision-making and debate.

Quality of debate

How can we deepen our connections? Within crucibles the quality of thinking and discussion is critical to developing maturity. Sometimes this needs to be structured or even provoked a little. Constructive challenge is a framework developed and promulgated by the author to encourage and allow challenge within decision-making in a reasonable and sometimes depersonalised way. It provides a structure or discipline for questioning that is both flexible as well as organised. These frameworks give permission for questions to be raised that might otherwise not be brought forward without fear of embarrassment, career detriment (at work) or social awkwardness. Surprise and humour can be introduced and are also useful.

Humanity necessitates handling complexity and nuance. Structured questions bring together the long term and the short, individual and collective perspectives, outcomes and process, the transcendent and the visceral, and theory and practice. One important aspect of a challenge framework lies in acknowledging responsibilities to self, peers, organisations, society and the environment. The process, we know, is not necessarily going to provide a right or ethical answer but might promote a more thoughtful and considered approach and lead ultimately to a more rounded solution. Maturing our Humanity involves having to deal with fine and delicate distinctions with high levels of uncertainty that often turn out to be important.

Example framework

1. Trust
   - Do others trust me / us? Should they?
   - How will this action foster trust and build relationships?
   - Under pressure do we swap co-operation for coercion?
   - Do we have a duty of care?
   - Do we apply ethical criteria to gain an advantage or because we believe it is right?

2. Openness
   - Are we keeping anyone in the dark - if so why? Who else should we involve?
   - How do we help others to understand us?
   - What do we do when no one is looking?
   - Would we be happy to have anyone from outside see this - including the press?
   - Is 'openness' only real only when someone asks us for information ...?

3. Fairness
   - Who benefits - and should they? Who loses out?
   - Would we be happy to give this advice/service to our families?
   - Is this how we would like to be treated?
   - Do we deliver what we say we will do? Do we stand by our commitments? Always?
   - Are we up to the job – or should we refer on?

4. Responsibility

> - What values define us?
> - Have we given enough 'space' to consider the ethical issues?
> - Do we give people enough space to choose to act ethically?
> - What is our key driver?
> - If we look hard - is there an implied or inbuilt prejudice here?

5. Sustainability

> - What are the effects of our actions on others in the short and the long term? How do we weigh these up?
> - Do we learn from our mistakes? How can we build-in resilience for the long term?
> - What does sustainable mean to us?
> - Does the status quo represent a fear of change, self-interest or the paralysis of a fear of failure? How do we deal with difficult questions?
> - Do we engage with others on sufferance, when we have to, or continually and with a purpose? Do we listen and learn?

Ethics

'Ye who are fed / By the dead letter, not the spirit of things'.
William Wordsworth, *The Prelude,* Book VIII

We have seen that within crucibles deepening maturity needs some encouragement through lively agitation, debate or constructive challenge. Part of that 'stirring of the casserole' comes from the injection or inclusion of the principles and constructs of ethics. Ethics is the systematic consideration of what we see as good and right – universal concepts that most of us hold as valuable or even true. Being mature usually involves becoming clearer about what our shared ethics are and more adept in handling them, evaluating them, and coming to conclusions using ethics on a reasonably consistent basis.

Ethics express the values underlying and connecting our humanity. Some ethics may be regarded as absolute truths and others may be seen as relative or situational. There will always be some degree of cultural context and variations in interpretation and application. Societies (and sometimes the world) needs to form a degree of consensus and certainty on how to operate ethics effectively or incorporate them into the law or international human rights. Formulating ethical views is often painfully slow and taxing. In many ways such a process ought to take time and be uncomfortable as they are dealing with fine distinctions and profound principles. Arriving at a workable degree of certainty is often an iterative and living process. We need the fine skills of being selective in our information gathering and then constructive in challenging ideas to produce rounded judgments. Ethics and principles become practice.

An Ethical Framework

Another form of constructive challenge is to challenge yourself on what you value.

This ethical framework was first designed by the author with colleagues to form the basis of The

Ethics Mark registered in 2004 to help organisations and communities or any number of us collectively to explore and uncover shared values based on ethics.

Here we offer some space to help you to work out your ethics and principles and what you want to connect to. What follows is a series of spaces (crucibles if you like) and questions to consider and respond to openly.

This document should also be updated and reviewed frequently.

1. Motivation or Purpose

Why do you do what you do? What drives joint actions and plans? What are you trying to achieve together?

What is your collective purpose? What is the wider impact of what you do? Why is it worthwhile? How do you express your aims, direction and principles? What really drives you? How do you strike a balance between prosperity, fulfilment, family, trust, and community commitment?

2. Finding your place in the Environment and Community

What do you do - both short and long term - to reduce your environmental footprint, combat climate change, increase biodiversity and help manage the environment? How do you engage and enable sustainability / ESG involvement within the local community?

Who do you regard as the community? How do you contribute to building local capacity and resilience? Can you explain your approach to sustainability and the practical actions that you take? How do you involve everyone in local decision-making and planning?

3. Using Ethics and Values

How do you collectively show or exercise your ethics and values every day with integrity? (i.e., consistently and when no one is looking)

How widely are values understood and shared in the community? How does the community develop common values and create the space day-to-day to do so? How are shared ethics recognised – or not? What steps are taken to educate, train, and motivate those across the community? What, if any, steps are taken to be even more inclusive and to deliberately help others to understand the values and ethics and the reasons behind decisions?

4. Fairness – and decision making

How do you all treat others in the community (as they would like to be treated)? How is fairness to all demonstrated?

Facing opposing pressures—quality, cost, integrity, deadlines, environmental impact, work or life balance, and many more – how are these balanced using ethics? It isn't always easy to reconcile obligations and be 'fair' to different parties. Can you show a direct link between shared values and ethics and decision-making and actions? Can everyone see this? Are you all happy to "own" your decisions? Do you sometimes put other's interests ahead of your own or make "brave" decisions? We all make mistakes, but far more is revealed by how we deal with them. How do you deal with the inevitable mistakes and concerns?

5. Independence and authenticity

How do shared ethics and values help in dealing with conflicting pressures and interests in and between communities? How does your community provide leadership? Who do you inspire? How do you demonstrate authenticity?

How do you or the community take a stand? How does it innovate or push the boundaries in respect of ethics? In what ways do you seek to influence the values of others outside your community and the ethical climate in which you operate? How do you build community understanding and skills? Whom do you motivate by what you do or how you do it? What do you want others to see you are committed to?

The Trouble with Ethics

No one is perfect,[1] indeed, far from it. There are few more irritating than the smug, the self-satisfied and 'goody goodies'. Orwell notes: '... on the whole, human beings want to be good, but not too good and not quite all of the time.'[2]

In so many spheres of life rather than follow rules to the letter we would do better to get under the skin of the detail and try to discern or appreciate the 'spirit' of things. Ethics can seem a vague and robust term at the same time. It combines what seem to be the constants of common humanity with a flexibility that allow sensible and practical interpretations and applications to fit a range of circumstances. This necessary flexibility can have the effect of undermining and devaluing the underlying strength of ethics. Flexibility does not have to mean weakness or corruptibility, in the same way as consistency of principle should not squeeze out adaptability or discourage innovation. The trouble with ethics is that establishing and using ethics can seem too difficult and, for those who yearn for simplicity or speed, ethics rarely offers up simple solutions ... Maturity usually requires making an effort with ethics.

---

[1] John Greenleaf Whittier, 'Dear Lord and Father of mankind, Forgive our foolish ways,' 1872, our wedding hymn. Adapted by Horder in 1884 and usually set to Repton by Hubert Parry.

[2] George Orwell, *The Art of Donald McGill*, 1941

Chapter 6
People

'The best things any mortal hath are those which every mortal shares.'

This epitaph to T. Arthur Leonard OBE is set into the rock halfway up Cat Bells in the Lakes. The founder of the Holiday Fellowship (HF) movement saw that hard-working men and women would benefit from a break in the fells. His vision transformed the lives of many, including my mother's, travelling up from North London to Eskdale between the wars. It was she who introduced me to the hills (Hope Valley in the Peak District) aged 6. Later, I was delighted to work for HF as a walking leader, assessor of new leaders and a mapmaker in the Lakes.

    A community scheme in Grasmere to re-build our primary school aroused diverse passions. Overly ambitious plans proved too contentious, but it was possible to see in microcosm how community works and sometimes doesn't. The experience led me to propose, as then chair of the British Standards (BSI) Sustainable Development committee, a framework to help develop communities sustainably - standard BS8904. The concepts were subsequently taken forward by the International Standards Organisation (ISO) and ISO37101 was, suitably, finalised at an ISO plenary hosted in Grasmere. *The author is now seeking to initiate a parallel framework for rural communities and is co-chairing ISO's Co-ordination Committee on the wider framework of ESG (Environment, Social and Governance).*

Kinder Communities

How can we develop connections collectively and begin to measure success? Communities are a form of crucible. Healthy, balanced, welcoming communities are a product of human maturity and so they both assist and are a key outcome of deepening our collective humanity. Here we, only superficially, consider the contributors to success and suggest appropriate overall measures of success for sustainable, and resilient communities. As Pope Francis has highlighted:

> Today we can recognise that we fed ourselves on dreams of splendour and grandeur and ended up consuming distraction, insularity and solitude. We gorged ourselves on networking and lost the taste of community. We looked for quick and safe results, only to find ourselves overwhelmed by impatience and anxiety. Prisoners of a virtual reality, we lost the taste and flavour of the truly real. The pain, uncertainty and fear, and the realisation of our own limitations, brought on by the pandemic have only made it all the more urgent that we rethink our styles of life, our relationships, the organisation of our societies and, above all, the meaning of our existence.
> 'Fratelli Tutti,' *The Holy See*, 3 Oct. 2020, para 33

Community, or at least its basic fabric, naturally arises from a group of people living and working together in a place. This living together in relative proximity is a form of crucible that over time leads through shared experiences to a natural level of inter-dependence and mutuality, a common vision, shared structures, interests and values and often brings a sense of belonging and identity. A way of life springs up from the practical realities - the continuity of contact, the shaping of the landscape, the shared engagement of work and pleasure. Community is not just family and friends, or our proximate neighbours, but the people we pass habitually in the street, meet in the local shop, who deliver our post, milk and parcels, healthcare workers at the local surgery or hospital, bus drivers, our children's teachers etc. We connect with all of these and many more. The essence of community is not necessarily similarity but getting on with those who are different and rubbing along with everyone.

Grasmere case study

A study of our local village (and others) suggests seven key components of success:

- Services
- Economy
- Social infrastructure
- Governance
- Resilience
- Sustainability
- Well-being and spiritual value

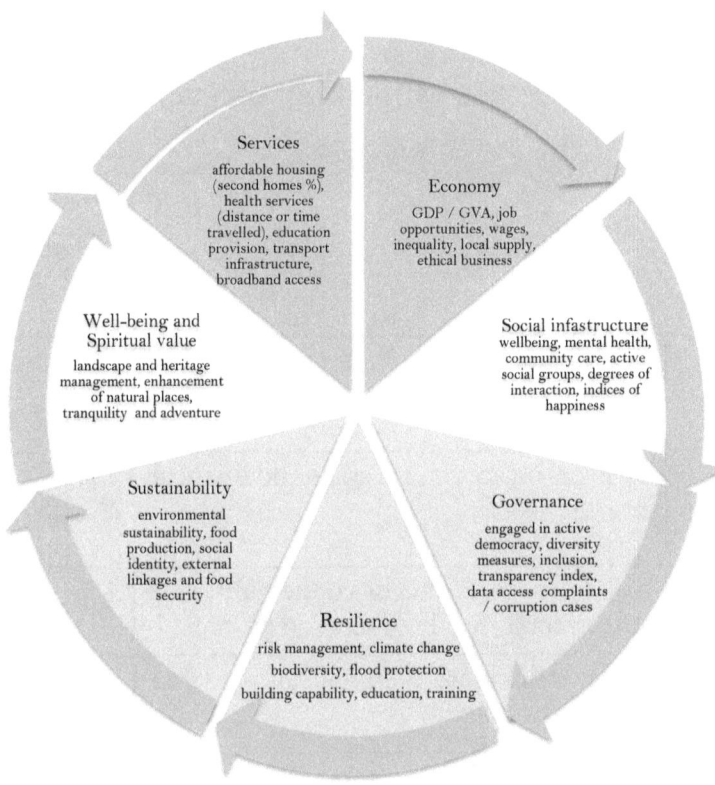

Note: Economy and Services are here linked to belonging. Governance, Resilience and Sustainability are linked to finding good. Social infrastructure and well-being are linked to caring for others.

How is your community doing?

A self-test to see how we think our community is doing.

		1	2
1	The values of community are not prominent in every day here.		
2	We focus on short term goals and financial returns.		
3	We don't have much connection with other people, live lives separately.		
4	Organisations are hierarchical, parochial and run by a few.		
5	Initiatives are hard to start and change is frowned upon.		
6	We feel dependent on external direction and interventions.		
7	We take things for granted. We don't put in more than we take out. We rarely consider 'why'.		

3	4	→
		We think about the values of community and are prepared to prioritise them, even if they may 'cost'.
		We see a longer term view and balance outcomes for all groups. We try to use local firms when we can.
		We join in, meet, support and look out for each other.
		We are open, inclusive, diverse, outward-looking and co-operative.
		There is a local 'spirit' of empowerment, of trying new things and encouraging learning and creativity.
		We are confident in our own values, we are OK with constructive challenge from each other and decide for ourselves what will happen in our area.
		We invest in people, recognising our interdependence and environmental responsibilities - including an understanding of 'why'?

Total the scores or consider as a 'profile'.

Also ask:

1. What are your community's skills?
2. How can we help each other?
3. What issues do we face?
4. What are our priorities for action?

Examples of local issues

(a)   Tourists who are attracted by the landscape may purchase second homes, pushing the price of small and family-sized houses beyond the reach of locals, particularly young people. Some of the second homes are used for two weeks a year leaving the community dead for much of the time. In Grasmere, it is estimated that 50% of houses are second homes or holiday cottages; in the neighbouring Langdale it is nearer 85%.

(b)   Services such as shops, buses, doctors, churches and schools also consequently find it hard to hang on due to lack of demand. Population demographics become skewed. It is a long journey to essential services such as hospitals. Low populations will also mean low investment from outside and slow broadband (although there are specific schemes locally to tackle this). Such areas are rarely attractive for new inward investment to diversify employment while policies made in metropolitan centres focus on what rural areas can do for them – food production, water supply, lungs (rewilding) or escapes.

(c)   Tourism is an essentially self-centered activity, taking experiences and selfies rather than contributing to the community. Incomers often bring their supplies with them and therefore there is little opportunity for mutuality or circular economies. Some buy local products, but the local economy becomes dependent and stultifies with few quality opportunities beyond tourism and farming - both paying lowish wages. Consequently, young people feel they have no option but to leave. Hidden loneliness and the consequent stress can be unexpectedly high.

(d) Wealth is disproportionately concentrated in the hands of older generations (a form of intergenerational inequity). This limits the vision for change (existing residents want to keep their idyll as they like it) and reduces community resilience and adaptability and overall sustainability.

Principles for kinder communities

Mutuality is derived from the fact that a group of people, through co-operation, are better able to act for their mutual benefit than if acting alone. From this simple but central tenet, comes the overarching objective of mutuality: namely, that mutual businesses and societies seek to benefit their members' quality of life rather than maximise profit.

Shared external relationships make a community open to outside ideas, people and contributions while balancing new and existing links and traditions. The aim is responsible relationship to support other communities.

Sense of locality/place implies putting into as well as

taking out of the community. This means appreciating what is distinctive and special about the local area, for example landscape, biodiversity, architecture and heritage. Cultural traditions in the area are also important in giving and defining an area's character.

Shared use of community space e.g. playing fields, commons, schools, community buildings and meeting spaces, streets. Local ownership and stewardship of land and assets through local trusts or in the UK, Community Interest Companies (CiCs), etc. An easy way for local people to work together.

Connectedness means close interaction between economic, social and environment interests. Having a good understanding of how interdependent all issues are and how solving problems in one aspect can have positive and negative knock-on effects. This also allows for finding win-win-win scenarios; achieving economic prosperity, but at the same time bringing about social progress that is sensitive to protecting and enhancing (rather than damaging) the environment.

Engagement and inclusivity – Inclusive participation emphasises the importance of good governance based on strong democratic principles – differences are mediated and resolvable in the open. There has to be accountability to the wider community as well as empowerment to help the community develop confidence in working out what matters to them, their values, and their own capabilities to help find solutions with others. Respect for all members in the community is necessary – all are treated with dignity and encouraged to belong and participate.

Localism – 'we do what we feel is right for our community' - not at any cost i.e. ensuring environmental and social justice across neighbourhood:
- Empathy and understanding of others' needs and aspirations
- Coherence of vision
- Strengthening and promotion of local identity through mutuality and reciprocity
- Using local schools, shops, working near-to-home, mutually supportive neighbours
- Tolerance and patience to find community based, practical solutions

Intra-community equity is the principle of promoting equity between and within different communities and groups. It implies that consumption and production in one community should not undermine the ecological, social, and economic basis for other communities to maintain or improve their quality of life.

Intergenerational equity is the principle of equity between people alive today and future generations. Unsustainable production and consumption by today's society will degrade the ecological, social, and economic basis for tomorrow's society, whereas sustainability involves ensuring that future generations will have the means to achieve a quality of life equal to or better than today's.

Quality of the environment at the local level can be mapped, protected and improved. Local planning decisions reinforce environmental quality and protect biodiversity "goods". A functioning environment provides clean air, water and fertile land to support communities.

We all accept we need to be less wasteful, be more resource efficient, reduce our consumption. This will help ensure sufficient resources, especially natural and non-renewable ones, are available for future generations.

Resilient and adaptable communities are capable of bouncing back from adverse situations and changing the way things are done to respond to the changing circumstances. It means not only protecting against negative impacts, but also making us better able to take advantage of any opportunities. When times are bad they can call upon the myriad of resources that make them a healthy community. A high level of social capital means that they have access to good information and communication networks in times of difficulty and can call upon a wide range of resources.

Resilience to difficulties and threats includes economic downturn and natural disasters, such as flooding, droughts, fires, disease (including pandemics), scarce and limited access to food and fuel.

Thriving economy – diverse training, skills and job opportunities: for those who are unable to gain paid work, being meaningfully engaged and fulfilled contributing to society in their local neighbourhood, through voluntary and community informal activities.

Affordable housing – designing homes and spaces for lifetime needs, reducing the need to move. Consideration of co-housing for existing and new developments, intergenerational, young and old interacting and supporting each other.

Capacity and capability in knowledge and know-how and skills that is shared and extended within and across neighbourhoods. Capability and competence audit and shared. Collective values are shared and communicated with learning and broader community education and empowerment of the community.

Constructive challenge in communities
Constructive debate and challenge is useful in a healthy community to ensure a better quality and more rounded and inclusive decision-making.

Suggestions of questions to ask, from any standpoint, based on the seven dimensions of success that emerged from the Grasmere case study:

Services	
	How can we enable young people/key workers on low pay or in their first job or perhaps with young families to find suitable and affordable accommodation locally?
	How can we help local home-owners not feel they have to sell to the highest bidder? (usually from outside for second home)
	What levels of services make a population viable? How long to get to a doctors, hospital, chemist, police station, or maternity unit is acceptable?
	Do we have enough support and care in the community for mental health care?
	How far is it acceptable to travel to the local school, shop, pub, garage, bus stop, supermarket, butchers, bank, open space?

Economy	
	How can young and older people find suitable jobs locally to avoid them leaving the area to move to the cities?
	What percentage of job opportunities are higher level, skilled roles?
	What is the average wage? GVA? GDP? How could productivity be improved? What % of working population are on minimum wage or zero-hour contracts?
	What training is available locally for needed jobs?
	What % of supply chains are / can be sourced locally?
	What % of local businesses are ethical, organic, fairtrade?

Governance	
	What % of population engage in the democratic process? e.g. average turnout, diversity, age groups, % occupying roles in local government
	How is the electorate communicated with between elections?
	How long do average councillors serve? And post holders in local societies?
	In voluntary groups, schools, churches etc how diverse is the representation on organising committees etc.
	How are local planning and development actions consulted on?

Social Infrastructure	
	How many informal contacts made per citizen per day? (survey)
	How many clubs and societies engaged in by average citizen? Hours per week given to local causes?
	Levels of loneliness and stress Suicide and indebtedness rates
	What engagement in local celebrations, festivals, events per year? Numbers involved? Significance outside area
	How much funding raised locally for local issues/care? e.g foodbanks
	Sense of belonging / place / identity (survey)

Wellbeing and Spiritual values	
	What places are held to be of local value and identity?
	Where do people go to find tranquility / solace? How are these places managed and protected, if necessary?
	What are the landscape / waterscape qualities? Where do visitors travel from?
	How does the environment offer opportunity for adventure, challenge, investigation, imagination and adrenalin-junkies?
	How do we connect with our heritage here?
	What does 'place' mean to locals and visitors? (survey)

Sustainability	
	What is the role of the countryside? Is it enough to be a food producer, or an outsiders' playground?
	How is the rurality of the area helping to combat climate change?
	What is the future of farming in helping the environment?
	What is our sense of identity with our landscape?
	What % of waste goes to re-cycling or landfill %? Are there plastics in water bodies? What are pollution levels? Are there invasive species?

Resilience	
	What risks does the community face in the short and long term?
	What is the community doing itself to take responsibility for building its capabilities and capacity?
	How can we increase or protect biodiversity?
	How often do we review our plans?
	What innovations are we exploring?
	Do we have an up-to-date audit of our community?

Measuring success
Our focus should be the aggregated outcomes of maturity – the experiences of everyday lives in practical terms that come from countless individual decisions and systems in communities. A useful tool for assessing maturity is the maturity matrix which can be constructed and maintained for an organisation or a community.

Maturity matrix
An indication of how a maturity matrix might be structured is suggested below. The elements and four Stages shown are intended for guidance and illustration only and are not exhaustive. All the cells could be quantified but that would require significant further research.

Examples of maturity matrices co-developed by the author can be found in British Standards on sustainability, the BS8900 series and especially the BS8904 guidance for sustainable communities. International standards have followed, the ISO37101 series and especially the guidance of ISO 37104 and 37111 are useful and have maturity matrices.[1]

In many ways the maturity matrix below summarises the key principles and outcomes of ESG (Environmental, Social and Governance) measures that the author is currently seeking to advance as co-chair of the ISO (International Standards Organisation) Coordination Committee on ESG.

---

[1] Copyright BSI and ISO see https://www.bsi-group.com/en-GB/

Some of the current issues affecting communities include:

- Vulnerable groups and reducing harm
- Modern-day slavery
- Intergenerational equity
- Supply chain standards
- Transition to net-zero or climate adaptions
- Use of plastics
- Diversity, equity and inclusion
- Responsible (ESG) investment and green finance

For all of these, especially the social issues, credible measurement, reporting and verification is all important if progress is not to be undermined by a lack of fair dealing (greenwashing for example) leading to an erosion of trust.

Kinder communities – maturity matrix
Here are some simple examples based on Grasmere (please add data for your own community)

	Stage 1 – Minimum standards	Stage 2 - Compliance
Belonging - Services	Shrinking population Many second or holiday homes Few shops, schools, post offices, banks Public transport intermittent or difficult	Stable population Most core services viable Second homes undermine locals' ability to find suitable housing
Belonging - Economy	Few job opportunities Outbound commuting Little inward investment or enterprise	Some economic diversification and support e.g. high speed broadband, 5-year plan Active job market, flexible, productive employment
Finding good governance	Closed or siloed structures and mentality Limited collective activity or outreach Unimaginative use of resources	Local newsletter/website Governance is often reactive and cautious Maybe decision-making dominated by a small group

Stage 3 - Commitment	Stage 4 - Values led
Co-operative schemes to boost or rescue key services Affordable housing accessible Sensible travel times/cost to hospitals etc	Expansion of younger, diverse population Multiple housing types and prices for rent/buy Sharing of services support for local shops, pubs etc
Sustainable job market with a range of wages and roles Building re-use Cooperative planning	Buoyant wages Accessible career development Credit unions / community companies Leaders' networks
Active local supportive political engagement Community centres and varied use of public spaces Curating heritage	Grass-roots initiatives, self-led, inclusive Sharing learning and leadership outside the community

	Stage 1 – Minimum standards	Stage 2 - Compliance
Finding good - Sustainable	Limited view of external stakeholders Limited standards for sustainability or environmental impact and biodiversity Low engagement from business community	Farming more diversified Recycle, reuse, repair Preserving some sensitive ecosystems Business planning together Events for local suppliers
Finding good - Resiliance	Lower life expectancy Deprivation Inequality Limited support for vulnerable	Statutory provision only Limited care in the community
Care - Social infrastructure	Fragmented or isolated / weak self-help networks Cultural and social activity limited Loneliness and stress	Societies, clubs, faith centres, teams emerge Community does come together except for major festivals Some limited shared vision or initiative
Care - Wellbeing and spiritual values	Unchanging culture; may be driven by some privileged groups Poor development of culture / values Little focus on creative skills and enterprise	Some, often tourist related, arts / crafts Emerging well-being focus for individuals only Limited awareness of value of area / heritage

Stage 3 - Commitment	Stage 4 - Values led
Outside funding attracted Stronger eco-relationships Businesses contribute to local causes and have stronger community embeddedness	Diverse land use models Businesses give local staff latitude to contribute and volunteer / engage for community good
Environmental and climate activism, reducing plastics Community audit Some awareness and support for vulnerable groups	'Building in' resilience / good mental health / self-help and training Public services meet needs of vulnerable
Local supply chains Good neighbour schemes e.g. food banks, young and older peoples' clubs	Collective energy schemes Car sharing schemes Close involvement in schools and training
Arts festivals, keep traditions alive Saving key buildings Create new open spaces Focus on mental health	Authentic 'buzz' Variety of arts opportunities An accessible and valued landscape and culture Obvious sense of place

Charter

'When Adam delved and Eve span,
Who was then the gentleman?'
    Rev John Ball, 7th June 1381, executed in Smithfield after the Peasants' Revolt

The Challenge

How can maturity become part of daily life? The Charter is one form of 'portable crucible' that encourages constructive challenge and can be utilised especially in our communities.

How do we translate sound theory about belonging, good and love into practice? How do we share sound habits and build cohesiveness and collective vision in our collective narrative and political life? One way maturity can be developed is by promulgating and using this New People's Charter. It promotes or creates an energy within any social, economic or political crucible – see Chapter 4.

The Charter came from conversations between the author and Rev Canon Cameron Butland, drawing on the social heritage of the Lake District and was first launched in the House of Commons in 2008, following the MPs' expenses scandal. Many world figures and local friends have signed the Charter.

The Chartist Movement 1838 - 1848

We are conscious of the historical precedence for a charter. The Chartist movement of the nineteenth century in Britain was one of the most influential mass political movements and created in many ways the outlines of our modern parliamentary democracy.

There were three Charters but the most influential was presented to parliament on 10 April 1848, signed by 6 million people. The Charter brought about five specific changes, eventually:

- Voting by secret ballot in all elections
- MPs not required to own property
- MPs to be paid
- Electoral districts to be of equal size
- Universal male suffrage

Chartism demonstrated the effectiveness of principles of democracy for a newly articulate middle and working class. Leaders such as William Lovett and Fergus O'Connor were the pioneers of community leadership. The Chartists were a genuine mass movement, showing how social maturity can develop. We re-imagine how a charter might look today.

Our shared challenges today

In the 21st Century we face serious issues such as growing inequality, globalisation, climate change, autocracy and pandemic – to name but a few. How does our essential humanity come into play and provide us with, perhaps, our best hope for a sensible and sustainable future?

As the 19th Chartists lent weight to a wide range of collective movements for social justice - among them the Labour party, the Co-operative movement and the football league – could grass-roots endeavour do something similar again? Not necessarily with a series of specific demands, but by fostering wider engagement in addressing human challenges in an open and inclusive way.

In an interdependent world everybody's values and ethics affect more people through social media - we are all so obviously inter-connected and all potentially have a voice – and therefore we need structures and processes that enable us to share those values safely, discover common ground and hopefully go on to create new meanings and positive outcomes - for everyone.

We can learn from the Sufi tradition of 'The Caravan of Creation' where those who have lived in previous generations have set out everything before us, and those yet to be born travel behind us, as it were in our footsteps. Is maturity of humanity more than a movement or perhaps the learning of good habits and a continual, contagious process of enabling a series of small steps by everyone in everyday action?

How do we help engagement in the maturity process embed? How can we stimulate the necessary constructive challenge to help us face complex problems and find new ways forward? One of the obstacles is the seeming unwillingness of some to listen to other viewpoints or even allow them to be aired. So-called 'cancel-culture' can hardly be conducive to wider maturity.

The Charter aims to turn strategic issues into specific questions that can be raised at every opportunity and scale – international, national, and community, corporate, family and individual – to help the maturity process. The Charter aims to help wrestle with significant underpinning themes such as responsibility, sustainability, inequality, marginalisation, globalisation and demographic pressure and then to signpost ways forward to deal with these working together.

The Charter is positive about our common future and is divided into ten commitments, each of which requires not simply assent but also action. By formulating the Charter in this way, it is hoped to give a simple, easily understood ethic as the focus for a much deeper and open discussion about what ethics, humanity and human maturity mean.

In 1848, six million people signed a charter that ultimately changed the world. Again, we need to do things differently. Consider the statements and questions below. If they resonate with you, sign The Charter and use it in decision-making and actions, and pass it on.

A New People's Charter

1. Face tomorrow's challenges today
What is our legacy?
Are we fulfilling the trust future generations place in us?

2. Stand responsible for our actions
Are we mature enough to be accountable for our choices?
How can we educate others to do the same?

3. Recognise when enough is enough
When is it time to stop?
Is it enough to simply live for ourselves?

4. Match our consumption to contribution
How can excess and poverty be reconciled?
Who do we depend upon and who looks to us?

5. See the 'whole' among the pieces
How can we search out that which is greater than ourselves? How can we make a difference?

6. Belong to place and community
Where is 'home'?
How can we make our communities sustainable?

7. Risk uncertainty, creativity and diversity
What are we afraid of?
Fear diminishes us all; how do we empower others and ourselves?

8. Give up the notion that anyone is superior to anyone else
Why should anyone be more entitled or privileged than anyone else? Can we be less for 'Me' and more for 'Us'?

9. Turn our world inside out by seeing through the eyes of others
How can we be more open to alternative views?
Why do we have more in common than divides us?

10. Search out that which is greater than ourselves
What is the 'extra'?
How do we find the things of greatest meaning?
How do we redeem each other?

Signed: Date:

© Cameron Butland and David Jackman 2008

Part C: Why?

Chapter 7
Crossing the Stream

'There are in our existence spots of time,
That with distinct pre-eminence retain
A renovating virtue, whence ... our minds
Are nourished and invisibly repaired;
A virtue, by which pleasure is enhanced,
That penetrates, enables us to mount,
When high, more high, and lifts us up when fallen.'
William Wordsworth, *The Prelude*, Book XII, 1805

Christmas Day
Families and friends have come and gone. My plasma exchange is started when everyone has left. A relief nurse volunteered to leave her family and come in from Manchester. In the end it takes six hours to complete and she falls on a bag of used plasma, hurts her arm and is cleaning until midnight. Perhaps the worst Christmas for both of us.

Public service is commonly misunderstood. It is borne of principles and a discipline of selflessness, underlain by a sense of duty and real self-sacrifice. The NHS is an example of unconditionality in practice, in this case effectively from the state, the community; from us all to us all.

Imagining then, looking down Easedale, as I so

often do from our bow windows, with remnants of snow and bright spring sunshine, watching a robin dance, suddenly the view transforms in what Wordsworth would call our 'inward eye', the scene and the senses becoming brighter and more vivid, richer, arresting and seemingly reaching right into an inner being. It is most definitely beauty, perhaps one of the most scenic places in the land, but in looking do we see 'beyond' to things more 'real', more 'truthful', more lasting?

The Question

Why mature at all? Is it just that we wish to experience more belonging, good, love and care as we proposed in the Foreword – or is there something beyond these benefits that draws us forward? Part C will endeavour to explore this question.

Firstly, we need to examine what maturity is before we can have any sense of what going beyond maturity might mean. Is the maturity of our humanity a steady evolution or is there a significant step we move to a different level? Most development or maturity curves suggests a smooth, organic process (if averaged out) – usually starting slowly, then building momentum, and finally plateauing sustainably - but in this particular development curve, the maturity of humanity, is there an inflection that could suggest a more fundamental turning point when we are in some way stepping over a line and/or changing fundamentally?

Firstly, we will consider what constitutes maturity, then how this builds what we describe as a kinder society, and finally why this home is a worthwhile endeavour.

The critical change is between Stages 3 and

4 of the Maturity Model. The critical change is the emergence of the quality of *unconditionality* – giving without condition i.e. without expecting anything in return. There may, of course, be many other or associated changes along the maturity curve, but this possibly irrational and unworldly concept, above all, holds a central place in maturing our humanity. We cannot offer a body of research to support this view, but we shall simply point to the fact that so many of our historical narratives, epics, religious allegories and so on, when seeking to express the special and distinctive quality of humanity – perhaps even the spiritual quality of humanity – alight on such selflessness as a key attribute. It seems that it is the idea of unconditionality that distinguishes a fundamental shift in the balance between self and other. This is the core difference between the deepening commitment of maturity Stage 3 and the values-led, sustainable Stage 4. At this point the balance of interest between self and other shifts (crudely over a 50%: 50% split) so that we reach a place where we are prepared to put another's interests ahead of our own.

Unconditionality can also involve a cost. Real cost. It means when giving without expecting anything in return we are also not counting the cost. This is selflessness indeed and represents a radical shift in the basic instincts of a me-centred individualism. In a real way it turns everything that follows in life on its head. Such a critical shift in the criteria we apply allows the application of new principles and results in changing priorities and outcomes. It involves adjustments in status, relationships, and measures of success. In the course of deepening maturity our nature is thereby changed and, as we will see in Chapter 10, we eventually come to a different place.

The practical results of unconditionality include committing to others in a more reliable, authentic, and genuine way. In fact, unconditionality can be applied to belonging (with place as an example), good (focusing on ethical principles) and love/care (building sustainable communities) - as we have seen in Part B - in the following ways:

- indivisibility with a place that has roots and heritage intimately wound into the warp and weft of the life of a locality, close to its environment and culture, welded into identity and feelings of home where you feel you belong or hefted.

- committed deeply to principles in a rational, structured and disciplined way, such as conceptions of right, such as fairness or equality, putting the pursuit of these principles or causes above your own interests and may be at some cost.

- a deeper communion with people and communities, beyond kinship-type bonds, the intertwining of lives through inter-dependence, living and working together, helping each other with a good heart, building systems of mutual benefit, shared vision and common experience.

Wordsworth's 'spots of time' in time join together to form something which may constitute a fulfilled and meaningful life as unconditionality changes the rules of the game. It influences all that we do and how we do it. The signs may be kindness and caring, and rather old-fashioned ideas of self-sacrifice, duty and respect. Being prepared to pay a price is also the essence of integrity which can be seen as the fundamental requirement of being mature in work or professional life. Integrity is actually the defining feature of being professional and having true independence and, thereby, being trustworthy.

In a modern context, selflessness appears as the first principle of the seven 'Principles in Public Life' as set out in the UK by Lord Nolan in 1995 in the first report of the Committee on Standards in Public Life.[1] Happily, selflessness is not defined nor is there any attempt to explain it. We should and do all know. This is much like the associated principle of integrity which is also not defined but central to the UK financial services regulatory system and any credible regulatory framework. We do all have some idea what these core principles mean but rarely discuss them or test their application. Yet should any in positions of leadership in public life fall short of these principles it is immediately apparent and raises questions of accountability, openness and honesty that in turn can erode trust and credibility in society.

Importantly, the introduction and experience of unconditionality seems to change our overall place in the wider whole. The shift also seems to be generally irreversible. Once this line is crossed it is difficult to re-cross or revert to old ways, as if we do (and of course we will from time to time) we will seem inauthentic, lacking integrity, shallow and trivial – to ourselves and others. This irreversibility is why such a change seems

---

[1] Committee on Standards in Public Life, *The Seven Principles of Public Life* May 30, 1995. https://www.gov.uk/government/publications/the-7-principles-of-public-life.

so powerful. We have crossed a real line, such as a bridge or a stream...

Postscript
On the other side of the Newlands Valley, not far from here, lies Stonycroft Gill - between Rowling End of Causey Pike and Barrow to the north. A path runs down from Sail, one of the finest of fells, to the farms of Uzzicar, crossing the beck by a small stepping-stone. I often re-visit this spot. This is how I envisage 'crossing the stream'[2] amongst the fells that are such old friends.

---

[2] Our 1970's Abba favourite 'I'll cross the stream, I Have a Dream', an echo of more carefree, unselfconscious times.

Chapter 8
Mysteries

If I say [the answer] it becomes, whatever the answer, a different book.... I will it to remain a blur and to be uncertain, as I am of many facts of daily life. This isn't a philosophy of aesthetics. It's a particular trick I felt justified in trying because my theme was India. It sprang straight from my subject matter. I wouldn't have attempted it in other countries, which though they contain mysteries or muddles, managed to draw rings around them. Without the trick I doubt whether I could have got the spiritual reverberation going. I call it a trick but 'voluntary surrender to infection' better expresses my state.

E.M. Forster's letter to Goldsworthy Lowes Dickinson, 26th June 1924

Background
This, the last chapter settled, was finalised in a conversation with long-time friend Canon Rev. Cameron Butland over a radiator in Lowther Castle on a cold winter's morning when lockdown deprived us of tea and a warm seat inside.

I was sent to Sunday School aged 6, part of a growing and vibrant non-conformist church in my village whose youth camps eventually brought me to the Lake District. For balance, I later went up to the highest of High

Anglican colleges, established by the Oxford Movement in memory of John Keble (1792-1866). Now, unsurprisingly somewhere in the middle, we are part of Grasmere church (St Oswald's). Therefore, it is only appropriate that here we illustrate faith from a Christian perspective, yet this should in no way diminish the parallels we are aware of in many other faiths.

Is the step of unconditionality essentially spiritual? We cannot ignore this possibility, especially given E.M. Forster's comments above.

Many will happily say they have beliefs or espouse deeply held values, but they may or may not ascribe these as anything to do with faith. Many follow their beliefs and values without feeling any need to belong to a faith community.[1] However, it is apparent that unconditionality forms a central principle of most conventional faiths and religions, as does the importance of belonging, good and love.

Saint Julian of Norwich (the first recognised female author in English) saw God as all and in all. If we follow Saint Julian's vision that God is love and this love is within all of us, then none of our efforts could make him love us any more or any less and there is no need to earn his favour.[2] However, if we start from the position that mankind is inherently unworthy and separate from God (original sin), then we will need God's

---

[1] Grace Davie, *Religion in Britain Since 1945: Believing Without Belonging*, 1994

[2] Saint Julian of Norwich, *Revelations of Divine Love* c1373. 'All shall be well, and all shall be well, and all manner of thing shall be well.' *God is all and in all*: Ephesians 4:6 King James Bible and The Great Bible, 1539, 1 Corinthians 15:28

help to be 'saved'. Some might say this is religion setting up a problem to which only it can provide (and control) a credible answer. But in both formulations, it is God that reaches out to the us first[3] in an unconditional way.[4] Whether or not it is up to us to open the door[5] of our souls, the resultant relationship of willing discipleship and service[6] is likely to turn out to look remarkably similar to the outcomes we highlighted in Chapter 3 as indicators of Stage 4. In other words, what we are describing is a mature humanity.

Whether maturity is divinely inspired and assisted, or emanates from a shared human spirit, the outcomes are likely to be similar. Both result in relationships restored; with families, communities, societies, and the planet. The very fact that our humanity seems to be ordered around belonging, goodness and love, and unconditionally, may be the strongest argument for the existence of a divine or good guiding force.[7]

Places of worship are crucibles in themselves, as Forster identifies in his use of the Mosque and

---

[3] John 3:16 For God *so* loved ... (emphasis added)
[4] Romans 5:8
[5] The college chapel of Keble in Oxford houses one copy of Holman Hunt's *The Light of the World*, 1853-4 showing Christ at a door, holding a lantern waiting to be let in: 'Behold I stand at the door an knock ...' a door with the handle only on the inside.
[6] 'What can I give him, give him my heart' from 'In the Bleak Midwinter' a poem and hymn by Christina Rosetti c1872.
[7] Psalm 14:1 suggests 'foolish is the man who says there is no God'

Temple. Many practices and celebrations of faith offer a reservoir of rich language and comfort in times of trouble or joy. For example, at my mother's funeral we had the exquisite exposition of unconditional love in 1 Corinthians, Chapter 13 – [if I] 'do not have love, I have become a noisy gong or a clanging cymbal. ...I am nothing. ...I gain nothing (v 1-3 New American Standard Bible - foreshadowing the echoes of *Ou-Boum*). This passage also emphasises maturity... 'When I was a child, I spake as a child, I understood as a child, I thought as a child: but when I became a man, I put away childish things. For now we see through a glass, darkly ...' (v11- 12 King James Bible).

Similarly, our melancholic Easter wedding hymn, *My Song is Love Unknown* (Crossman after Herbert, 1664), wonders – '*love for the loveless shown, that they might lovely be. Oh who am I ...?*' – unconditional love made sacred through resurrection and a relationship, '*This is my Friend...*'. Unanswerable. Everything else is secondary. So, if unconditional love/belonging/good is the essence of a maturing humanity and the glue, cement or even the building materials of our lasting 'home', does this become a, even the, spiritual question – the driving force behind the celestial drama we see unfold in Chapters 9 and 10? Unknowable. This 'grace of the Universe' (*Vanya* - see Epilogue) would be to one-time college chaplain, the late Bishop Geoffrey Rowell (who, incidentally, introduced us to The Delhi Brotherhood Society, home for our passage through India), one of the great *mysteries*.

Chapter 9
The Power of the Dog

'Bright star, would I were steadfast as thou art—
Not in lone splendour hung aloft the night
And watching, with eternal lids apart,
Like nature's patient, sleepless Eremite,
The moving waters at their priestlike task
Of pure ablution round earth's human shores,
Or gazing, on the new soft-fallen mask
Of snow upon the mountains and the moors—
No--yet still steadfast, still unchangeable,
Pillow'd upon my fair love's ripening breast,
To feel for ever its soft fall and swell,
Awake forever in a sweet unrest,
Still, still to hear her tender-taken breath,
And so live ever--or else swoon to death.'
    John Keats, 'Bright Star' 1819. Noticed on a visit to Keats's Hampstead home followed by a service in St Botolph's, Bishopsgate, on the poet's 250th anniversary celebrations.

What drives maturity forward?
Humanity's path can seem dramatic, like Keats's bright star, arcing across the firmament – but such a bold trajectory needs energy to propel it. If unconditionality is a core of human maturity – through the deepening of belonging,

finding good and caring/love – does this provide the driving force, an electricity for human maturity? We can see traces of such an energy shining through from the past, the sheer vivid colour of Caravaggio's Beheading of Saint John The Baptist 1608 in Valletta Co-Cathedral in Malta radiates energy across the ages, as does the joyous graffiti of the Santa Marta district of Lisbon, or the life-bustle of the Old Hong Kong Ferries and the original HDBs of Tanjong Pagar, in Singapore. Some people are on their own 'forces of nature', my wife included. Humanity's energy is boundless.

So perhaps we should actively try to envision a society and economy that promotes, enables, - or at least allows for – the principles of a more human economy. How might that work?

The flow of the human values we have focused on might provide the energy in the following way:

1. we receive good, kindness or love from others;
2. such good encourages and enables us to give or pass on the same to others;
3. in turn they pass on the good freely to others...

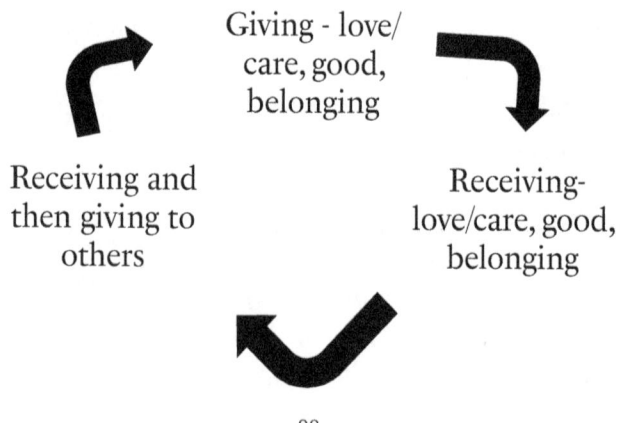

This flow creates, if we enable it, not just a virtuous circle but a continuous spiral of learning that drives creativity and maturity that together makes up a core of our Common Life.[1]

Seeing maturity as a collective endeavour, we can now see clearly how much we need each other for this flow of unconditionality and good to happen. Nothing of this nature can happen or progress without others willingly giving and receiving. A human economy is not individualistic or essentially competitive. It is not another 'zero-sum game' where if there are to be winners there must also be losers. Humanity is essentially a cooperative and collective effort with the flow of giving and receiving described above at least one element of the electricity that energises it. This potentially phenomenal explosive power, we have described elsewhere as reminiscent of the immense force of cavitation[2] that carves out cliffs, caverns and caves. Nothing lesser would even be capable of challenging or balancing the whole direction of conventional economies and societies as Smith describes them (see Chapter 2).

Searching for a kinder society is no naive prospectus; how we collectively, through a multitude of decisions and actions, large and small, move the corporate dial from unalloyed self-interest to a more

---

[1] *The Common* – a play by DC Moore enjoyed at the National Theatre 2017

[2] Cavitation in geomorphology is the immense energy released by the imploding vacuums within bubbles in the plunge pool of a waterfall. We see this energy daily in the waterfalls of Sour Milk Ghyll at the end of Easedale.

balanced and mature, values-led culture has been spelt out in the previous two volumes. ESG is one example – including concerns such as social equity, modern-day slavery, conflict minerals and vulnerable consumers, alongside climate change (incidentally, the subject of my first university tutorial as far back as 1978). The mechanism for change remains minute shifts in individual and collective understanding of the fine balance between self and other – the core of the journey of maturity described in this book from Chapter 2 to 7.

In summary, organisations, businesses, economies need to move from a solely self-serving focus on bottom-line profitability to evaluating and reporting their overall contribution, especially in terms of the external outcomes of their actions for everyday folk in their everyday lives. Just as we have seen for individuals and society, this requires a culture-shift to more mature decision-making where ethical and community values and principles are internalised to the extent that all throughout an organisation *want* to support a broadly 'kinder society'.

If 'in search of a kinder society' is reasonable shorthand for the product of maturity, we must also understand those who want none of it. Undoubtedly, some will get stuck at Maturity Stage 2, because risk-managed, mechanical compliance is so comfortable and box-ticking launders conscience. Others seem to enjoy blocking the flow of kindness, possibly to sate an endothermic vanity. Some will subvert selflessness, disguising self-absorption by incessant virtue-signalling, while a few seek to exploit kindness and oppress, viciously. It is a drama that echoes *The Power of the Dog* (2021 film and 1967 book of the same name, referencing the climactic Psalm 22).

Chapter 10
Coming Home

'Once there was a way to get back homeward...
... in the end
The love you take
Is equal to the love you make.'
Extracts from 'Golden Slumbers/Carry That Weight/The End' 1969 the final recordings by The Beatles, Abbey Road. 'Golden Slumbers' is partly from a lullaby by Thomas Dekker, 1599 Copyright Sony/ATV Music Publishing LLC 1969

New Year's Eve
The lantern of Liverpool's Catholic cathedral glints between the skeletons of unfinished hospital buildings – a light in the darkness. Surely, we can settle on some meaning here. From this bed I have wondered if there can be anything redeeming. Yet countless acts of kindness, comfort and love spill out. May be we've found a form of redemption in the practice of belonging, finding good and love; and receiving and giving unconditionally. We end up in a place that we have made, an 'other', and an 'all'.

The last stage

We have found at every turn that we cannot mature alone – we need each other to love and be loved, to find good and to belong. We have to mature together. The final element of maturity, which also has to be a collective effort, is receiving with good grace. That is without any sense that the giving and the gift are deserved or earned, or indeed the result of a pursuit by the receiver. Nor does the receiver need to feel they are worthy of the gift nor, on the other hand, should they feel any guilt or debt or the need to repay; the kindness is freely given.

If receiving is another form of unconditionality, who is maturing, the unconditional giver or the receiver? In Chapter 9 we saw how it is not only in giving to others that we find fulfilment, but it is also true that the receiver finds fulfilment in a graceful acceptance. There are many examples throughout that to be fully mature we need to be both giver and receiver.

This sense of a proper and wholesome understanding of such grace extends to accepting ourselves, our situation, our role, our family and friends as well as all the good things around us, the opportunities that open up, the risks and responsibilities that challenge us and the colour of life in all its richness; a felicity[1] that comes from living life to the full.

The end of the journey

Countless maturity decisions lead us, whether purposefully or incidentally, to build our 'human home'.

Now we can see the sweep of maturing humanity and pick out three key steps:

---

[1] Thomas Traherne, poet (1637 –1674)

1. Connecting – with others, such as belonging, finding good and loving/caring.
2. Unconditionality – putting the interests of others before our own.
3. Grace – receiving freely, without presuming or deserving.

Each step involves increasing degrees of selflessness, a shift from an inward focus to an appreciation and care for others and beyond as we sought where we began in Chapters 1 and 2. Each step of the way develops and embeds the three core elements we identified from the beginning – belonging, good and love / caring.

We started there from a lonely individualism, slowly recognising and connecting with the others we find matter most, deepening those connections into more unconditional commitments, and as we learn to receive gracefully in the same self-less way, our humanity becomes more fully mature. However, the journey is not sufficient in and of itself, and nor are the benefits of maturity - experiencing a deeper sense of belonging, good and love. Something else of value lies beyond that draws these threads together. As we mature we change and change others around us - as we help each other along. We create together 'places' – we might speak of, like Wordsworth (Chapter 7), moments in time and space - which are different in nature and value.

We could call such places 'home'.
Wordsworth saw Grasmere as a perfect home:

> 'A Whole, without dependence or defect,
> Made for itself and happy in itself,

Perfect Contentment, Unity entire.'
William Wordsworth, 'Home at Grasmere' 1814

Again, home is not about us as individuals or what we have become, but the outcome of the deep connections we have made with others along the way, and what we then naturally create collectively. This home that draws us on is the end of our journey.

As Forster recognises, this is the conclusion of the... 'search of the human race for a more lasting home' [2]

Ou-Boum

Ou-Boum is the pivotal expression of E. M. Forster's *A Passage to India* and is used to describe the enormity of the monotonous echo that reverberates around the Marabar caves. Both parts of this haunting proclamation are critical, holding in tension both options open to us. This clause sets up the central axis of our humanity and thus the theme of this book. Boum reminds us of the sheer pain, sadness and loneliness of the vast universe, the utter emptiness of nothingness. Nihilism may seem an attractive opt-out here[3] but there's either a story or there isn't.

Ou, reflecting the Buddhist and Hindu 'Om', suggests another option, a place formed from the wholeness of everything good in humanity. *Ou-Boum* is literally ....

... 'Everything and nothing at the same time.'[4]

---

[2]   E.M. Forster, 'Three Countries' manuscript.
[3]   As discussed entertainingly in the film *Everything Everywhere All At Once*, 2022
[4]   A Facebook comment on *A Passage to India*

If we seek to answer the 'why?' question simply in terms of how the maturity journey benefits us; that is in terms of self-fulfilment, quality of life, duty, some contrived purpose or destiny, meaningfulness or comfortable wellbeing, we have missed the point entirely. We fall at the final hurdle, and again delude ourselves.

Boum blows such self-indulgence away:[5]

> Pathos, piety, courage—they exist, but are identical, and so is filth. Everything exists, nothing has value. If one had spoken vileness in that place, or quoted lofty poetry, the comment would have been the same—"ou-boum" ... no one could romanticise the Marabar because it robbed infinity and eternity of their vastness, the only quality that accommodates them to mankind.[6]

The Marabar Caves represent Forster's central crucible. It is here that his story turns, based on the choices his characters make. But Forster's journey has no elegant resolution:

> But the horses didn't want it – they swerved apart; the earth didn't want it, sending up rocks through which riders must pass single file; the temples, the tank, the jail, the palace, the birds, the carrion, the Guest House, that came into view as they issued from the gap and saw Mau beneath: they didn't want it, they said in their hundred voices, 'No, not yet,' and

---

[5] This brings to mind Verdi's *Requiem, II Dies Irae* or Puccini's *Tosca*

[6] E. M. Forster, *A Passage to India* p. 160

the sky said, 'No, not there.'[7]

Ou echoes back, speaking of the whole, the other, that which is beyond ourselves. In maturing we contribute to, and become part of, this wider good, that is substantive and lasting. This promise has pulled us forward throughout our journey, and taking us beyond death, something from nothing. A redemption.

Narratives of faith may help us comprehend this whole by replacing 'good' with 'God'. Wordsworth, who describes an *Ou-Boum* experience on Grasmere in *The Prelude*, prefers a focus on Nature: 'nature was to me then all in all', 'My heart leaps up when I behold A Rainbow in the sky', and 'I have learned to look on nature...hearing oftentimes the still, sad music of humanity', while Ruskin sees clearly 'poetry, prophecy and religion, all in one'. But we need not see the 'other' as a 'Vision Glorious', apart and above, we all know and recognise this place only too well. We have been there.

Ou-Boum, the tension between self and other, runs through our lives and through this book, tragedy and redemption sit side by side. The conscious and deliberate maturing of our core humanity gives us more and better ways of resolving this dilemma, but we gain heart from the surety of our starting propositions, also expressed by Wordsworth in *The Cumberland Beggar* (*Lyrical Ballads* 1800) and a letter to John Wilson (7th June 1802):

'We have all of us one human heart' ... and ...

'the greatest triumph of the human heart ... [is] the strength, disinterestedness, and grandeur of love'.

---

[7]   E. M. Forster, *A Passage to India* p. 316

And this is our hope, that by building out belonging, good and love into that unknowable space, piece by piece, imperfect plank by muddled nail, a rudimentary raft, messy and partial, becomes a living structure that supports and heralds our collective humanity. A place, a home, born of our core humanity, a 'light that overcomes darkness', somewhere from nothing, a new creation ... Whether this is pitiful or beautiful, it is, perhaps, all there is.

⚜⚜⚜

So this is it. This is all we have. This hope of a more mature collective humanity may seem a modest enterprise, but it is fulfilling and gives expression to the core of our human nature. Somewhere in all our flailing inefficiency, we find a shared truth – a truth we would not have realised had we not made the journey together. This journey is the most important thing we do, perhaps the only important thing we do – and becoming more mature gives life and succour to our collective humanity.

Conclusion

We started with *King Lear*, and we end with him too. The unexpected death of his daughter Cordelia brings utter despair:

> 'And my poor fool is hang'd! No, no, no life!
> Why should a dog, a horse, a rat, have life,
> And thou no breath at all? Thou'lt come no more,
> Never, never, never, never, never!
> Pray you, undo this button: thank you, sir.
> Do you see this? Look on her, look, her lips,
> Look there, look there!'
> William Shakespeare, *King Lear*, Act 5, Scene 3

For a moment Lear holds out a vain, desperate longing, believing hope beyond hope, Cordelia still to be alive, so they can be together. In that short moment, and, perhaps, only for a moment, the foolish Lear is redeemed. And so may we be.

In all, we need each other; good spreads from giving and committing to others unconditionally, as well as receiving willingly in good grace, and in doing so we bond and belong and form our collective home - our colourful communities and our shared places. We do not seek out these connections only for ourselves but work to create the conditions or spaces for others to find their maturity with us. Our humanity becomes fully mature in forming these connections collectively. We find life is, by turn, feeble and tragic, hopeful and majestic. It is nothing else. In doing all this we redeem each other.

Ends

Epilogue

'our nature is to try and to never stop trying and then, in those last minutes, we will see that our lives are beautiful and dignified... We'll understand.'
   Simon Stephens after Chekhov, *Vanya* (2023)

Far Easedale – a final walk
There's a path that runs around the back of the orchard and is reached by a small wicket gate. The path is very dry and stony uphill at first, one half winding up to the Lion and the Lamb, the other heading for Far Easedale and Borrowdale. I habitually take the lower path, into a small birch and oak clearing and around the back of the farm next door. Here you can stand completely cut off from any habitation and out of sight. A perfect mixture of man and nature of centuries past. There are no sharp lines, no right or wrong, just a tumbling wall, old, barbed wire and a few rusted stakes. This is a place complete and a place beyond. Nothing else; this is it.

There is great value in repetition. Treading the same footsteps day after day imprints a place within you, so you become part of the very ground on which you walk. We do well to travel at the speed of the land. You learn from it every time and you, thereby, give back in some unknowable way. I walk this path in all weathers every day I am here. This is where composing and curating these pages started and ends.

The track winds higher between dry-stone walls and the valley opens up with bracken emerging lime green in the spring. The remains of a fulling mill race – first recorded in 1283 - lies beneath the churning waters of Sour Milk Ghyll. Dolerite sills criss-cross the green-grey Ordovician andesite making this section hard going, but the path is well-trodden by the local Herdwick sheep with their broad, wool-covered legs and heavily matted coats spattered with bright red and blue shepherd's smits. They are truly hefted to this place. Walkers trudge on.

A steep cleft narrows the path, pushing fellow travellers together. The temperature here drops a degree. The beck runs faster and noisily as it too tries to squeeze through. This is the change from cultivated in-bye to open fell. The balance shifts, we feel more on our own, at one with nature.

Far Easedale is a broad, confident glacial basin set between the ridges of Gibson Knott and Tarn Crag, sheer slabs and slices of rock. A natural crucible. More time for comfortable conversation allows the focus of the day to shift from the journey to home.

Finally, we come to a narrow wooden bridge. It is here that I usually turn round, taking a minute or two to lean on the smooth railings and watch the still waters run away... Some cross unthinkingly, but some knowingly. Why so? Well, hopefully here we can understand.

THE 7

MYSTICAL LAWS OF ABUNDANCE

A Guide from the Sages on Effortless Abundance

Sujith Ravindran

SUJITH RAVINDRAN

Readers may disseminate any part of text contained herewith for teaching, coaching or quoting purposes without the permission of the author. However, please do not reprint or publish the text contained herewith with the intent of reselling the content.

The author does not take responsibility for any misunderstanding or consequences that may arise out of interpretations or extractions of the text contained herewith.

2018 Sujith Ravindran

ISBN-13: 978-1775319702

DEDICATION

To my little son, Adya:

What can this father teach you? What I try to work out in my head, you already live out of your heart; fiercely authentic, fully aligned with the Universe, as infinite as space, as eternal as time. You are already the supreme example of one who attracts effortless abundance.

CONTENTS

PREFACE 01

0. INTRODUCTION 09

1. THE LAW OF EXCHANGE 21

2. THE LAW OF ECHO 39

3. THE LAW OF DETACHMENT 53

4. THE LAW OF EXPONENTIALITY 73

5. THE LAW OF NON-LOCALITY 91

6. THE LAW OF DHARMA 109

7. THE LAW OF INEXHAUSTIBILITY 129

EPILOGUE 145

ACKNOWLEDGMENTS

First and foremost, I am grateful to the Universe for;

- ❖ Showing me the way
- ❖ Giving me the courage to live truth, and
- ❖ For showering my life with infinite abundance

No acknowledgment would be complete without thanking my teachers who have gotten me on my true path. The infinite wisdom contained in the texts of the Upanishads – especially the *Tattriya Upanishad*, and the *Artha Shastra* from Chanakya, two texts from the Indian Mystical tradition – have guided me towards effortless abundance.

I am grateful to Camilla, my wife, for patiently holding space for me to be myself and undertake my inner journey.

Lastly, this manuscript would not have found its final form without the able assistance of Afroze Ali, Thomas Dachsel and Anuj Saxena, all outstanding professionals and generous in heart.

PREFACE

During each visit to my *Guru*[1], I would notice someone who would raise a question about not having enough or wanting more. One evening a lady with a little girl in her arms asked, "How do I attract abundance into my life?" She seemed like someone who had plenty, yet the struggle in her voice was evident.

"Align yourself with the Universe. The Universe is generous," the *Guru* replied supportively.

"The Universe needs us humans in order to channel It's abundance into the world. Take a pause and understand this." He paused. "You have an important role to play, my dear lady. We all have an important role to play. In your role as a mother, you are being a channel of abundance."

He shifted his eyes towards everyone. "Our job as humans is to channel the Universe's abundance into manifestation," he raised both palms towards the sky as he explained. "If there are no beings, there is no abundance. There is no wealth to be distributed, there is no love to be shared, there is no happiness to be grown."

The curiosity was evident within the packed audience. I also noticed doubtful faces in the crowd.

"For abundance to happen in our lives and around us, we need to fully align ourselves with the Universe. If we approach abundance as if it is a goal to be achieved, the function of the soul is not fulfilled. The more we are self-attuned to our deeper realms, and the more aligned our being is with the Universe, the more we attract abundance. The Universe – the realm of infinite

---

[1] A spiritual teacher of the Indian tradition

THE SEVEN MYSTICAL LAWS OF ABUNDANCE

possibilities – is ultimately the home of all abundance; its origin, source and nature. What better Source to align with than the innermost nature of you and of everything! So, being a channel of abundance is an exalted position," the teacher elaborated.

"So how do we practice alignment with the Universe?" One participant asked.

"Keep your faith in three things and abundance will follow," the *Guru* responded. Everyone was seated in the hall facing him listening intently.

"Always have faith in the goodness of others." His head gently bobbed up and down as he spoke. "Humans, animals, plants...every being is generous. Everything is generous. Nature is generous. The Universe is generous by design," he stated with a sweeping gesture of his hand.

"Everyone is filled with goodness. It is only when we are stuck in our self-preservation mode that our goodness goes to sleep. It is the condition of inner scarcity of the ego that holds us back from being generous." He spoke in his usual slow voice.

"Then we start asking questions like, 'if I am helping you, what's in it for me?' Or, 'if I am spending time with you, what's in it for me?'

"But there is a part within each one of us that is pure and unhurt. And that part is filled with love. That part is caring and generous. Believe in it. Believe that each one of us has that pure and unhurt part."

"That is one." He raised his hand and kept count.

"Two, always have faith in yourself," he lifted a second finger.

3

"You are divine. You are unique. Believe in your gifts. What you have to offer is special. Not any less."

"Trust your own purpose," he spoke slowly.

"Do not doubt, 'oh God, this is not bringing me abundance'". His words were measured. "I have made all these paintings and I still haven't become Picasso. Or, I am putting all this effort, I am putting my things out...and nobody is buying my stuff. Maybe this is not for me." After a pause he stated, "That doesn't bring abundance. Do not doubt yourself. That trust in one self and purpose is important."

"I don't care if somebody is going to pay me a penny or not," he spoke in an exaggerated voice. "I am absolutely convinced that God has brought me in this form in order to do this work, in order to live precisely the way I am living now, offering the things that God has abundantly given me to share. Zero doubt about it."

"That is number two," he counted off on his fingers.

"Lastly, have faith in the seven laws," he asserted as he scanned the room with his piercing eyes. He paused to make sure that his message sank in.

During the time I spent with him, I have always seen him, and his *Sevaks*[2], live those seven laws every day. Their every word and every action shone those laws.

*   *   *

In most parts of the world that I travel to, the path to abundance is considered an uphill one. Abundance is considered to involve a

---

[2] Volunteers or paid servers who offer service

good amount of sweat and a lifetime of hard labor. Some also carry the belief that when they gain abundance, someone else loses.

Hence the concept that abundance is actually achieved through refining our 'being' and aligning ourselves with the Universe goes counter to the above beliefs. That is why it is essential that we remind ourselves of the seven laws laid out in this book. They are meant to give faith in trusting the Universe and aligning ourselves with It.

The seven spiritual laws of abundance are laws practiced by the Indian *Rishis*[3] for thousands of years. In India, a text called the *Artha Shasthra*[4] from Chanakya explains how abundance works. The Vedas offer the science of how the Universe responds with abundance to human actions.

We are living in interesting times where existing ways of pursuing abundance are clearly not working for most of us. For most, their material life does not reflect the same inner abundance that they experience.

Like never before, people are faced with extended work hours, exhaustion, burnouts, and an unending struggle to make both ends meet. This has left many of us disillusioned and feeling trapped in this hamster wheel of toil, with no relief in sight. They struggle to pay their bills and feel blocked from following their hearts due to their material limitations. Yet others have given up this way of life in exasperation and stripped down their life in order to live a bare life.

---

[3] A word used to denote sages of the ancient Indian spiritual tradition
[4] An ancient Indian treatise on money, statecraft and policy

More and more people are listening to their calling. Like never before, they are deserting secure jobs in order to follow their passions. Many are giving up a life of certainty and security and are going for a life of purpose and meaning. Many today step out of their relationships because their relationships do not support their passion.

Yet their material world does not reflect the richness of their inner world.

This manuscript exposes the sacred wisdom from the Indian spiritual masters on how to shape a life that would draw abundance towards you.

For the past eight years, every year I have toured four continents offering around seventy public events on spiritual growth. I have made all those tours together with my family. In the tradition of my spiritual masters, I offer all the open events worldwide on a donation basis, and my family and I have received enough abundance to live in comfort and fully experience the joy of these tours. This has been the outcome of the practice of faith in the sacred wisdom laid out in this book.

Over the years, countless consciousness workers I have met have adopted these laws into their lives and gifted their services compliant with these laws. Each day, countless more are rapidly transitioning their lives into this way of living, and they have started to experience the lightness of true freedom in it.

Over the past few years, I have noticed another trend emerging. My audience would often ask me questions regarding my lifestyle. "How do you live your life free from money and yet so comfortably?" They want to know. Their fascination with the way my family and I live, gifting our services freely to all, was noticeable. Through their questions, the topic of the seven laws started to come alive.

And, before I knew, I was invited to offer talks on the seven laws. In recent years I have offered numerous talks worldwide on the seven laws. And then somebody came forward and suggested, "Sujith, you really need to compile all these laws into a pocket book and release it. Millions across the planet will benefit from it."

I trust you are one of them who will benefit from the laws laid out in this book.

*   *   *   *   *   *   *   *

0. INTRODUCTION

During my younger days I practiced for three years with a *Guru* who lived by a village near where I then lived. He used to live and practice in a small *ashram*[5] in the outskirts of the village. With an hour-long bus ride through some tiny roads and a short walk, you could arrive at the *ashram* from the nearest city.

The *ashram* never had a fencing around, so you never knew how much land it had. Cows and dogs from the village would go in and out of the *ashram* land, children were always playing noisily on its land, and on some days, it felt like the entire village was working on the *ashram*'s land. The *ashram* itself was a scattering of a few sheds with one large hall in the middle, the meditation hall.

Abundance is a part of a holistic process meant to meet the material and spiritual needs of all beings

I would often visit this *Guru* and stay with him to practice and listen to his spiritual fables. It is from his life example and teachings that I got my best grounding in the seven laws of abundance.

Whenever I visited the *ashram*, I would not be the only one there. Any given day, there would be five or six volunteers, twelve to twenty residents, and nearly a hundred visitors. Most of them arrived for the morning and evening *Satsangs*[6]. When I visited I would be amongst people of all races, old and young, men, women and children.

---

[5] A monastery in the ancient Indian tradition
[6] Spiritual discourses and practice sessions

THE SEVEN MYSTICAL LAWS OF ABUNDANCE

Many who visit the *ashram* never spoke the local languages, but that never mattered inside the *ashram*. Inside the *ashram*, everyone came together in a common bond of humanity. With a smile, a genuine interest in each other and plenty of hand gestures, everyone served each other. Every person was seen as a divine being on his or her own special journey. Nobody there cared about your faith or your sexual orientation. Every being was given the same level of respect. I cannot remember a single occasion when the *ashram* folks turned back any person who wanted a place to sleep or a meal to eat.

*   *   *

'*Atma mokshartham jagat hitayacha*' was written in bold letters at the entrance of every shed. It means 'Self-realization and Service to All'. This statement articulated the *dharma*[7] of the *ashram*.

The mindset was that abundance is a part of a holistic process meant to meet the material and spiritual needs of all beings, humans and beyond.

"**We are held in the planet as much as the planet is held in the galaxy**," the Guru liked to say.

Among all the residents, there was a profound understanding that we are an integral part of a greater sea and we exist in essential dependence on the broader environment. As we would take great care to wash and shampoo our hair, the residents would take great care to keep well their surroundings, the environment, other beings, and beyond.

"Our own practice and our service, that is why we exist," he

---

[7] The reason for existence

would constantly remind us. "The moment we are obsessed with finding love, or good health, or wealth, or anything else material, we have lost sight of our purpose."

"Don't worry about anything. All is taken care of. Our greatest calling is to live our *dharma*," he would often repeat to the residents and *Sevaks*.

And indeed, everything was taken care of in the *ashram*. There never was a lack of anything. There never was an alarm about anything being absent or unavailable.

Every hour of time in the *ashram* was made available to live the pure joy of giving.

The *Guru* or any of the *Sevaks* never ate until each person and animal had received their meals. Only after he was informed that all others have been served would he sit down to eat.

He never declined a request for an appointment by any spiritual seeker. When there was a practitioner who sought his presence, everything else could wait.

Sometimes I would see this *Guru* give the most exotic gift to the poorest of the lot. One day I saw him give away his handheld transistor radio to a homeless man. This homeless man was squatted on the floor next to the *Guru*'s seat, listening intently to the sound coming out of that box. His eyes were filled with wonder, and he looked at the shiny device as a miracle.

At one point, the homeless man could not contain himself. He asked the *Guru* if he could touch the radio. He then gently ran his coarse fingers over the knobs and the metallic body, completely thrilled by the experience.

THE SEVEN MYSTICAL LAWS OF ABUNDANCE

The next moment the *Guru* picked up the radio and gave it to the homeless man, "Keep it," he said. "It is yours."

The stunned homeless man gingerly took the transistor, looked at it with wide eyes, then held it close to his chest and giggled.

"Why did you give your transistor radio to that homeless man?" Later I asked the *Guru*. "He has no use for it."

"Really?" The *Guru* replied with questioning eyes. "Did you look at him? Did you see how excited he was?"

"It meant a lot more to him than to me," he casually added after a pause.

"And what about you? You liked to listen to the news on that transistor every day," I remember asking.

"No worries. Now let someone else listen to the news." He responded. "Giving, receiving, giving, receiving....that is how the world moves," he waved one hand in the infinity sign.

Though I was the only one who witnessed the *Guru* gift the radio to the homeless man, I never spoke about it to anyone associated with the *ashram*. The next time I visited the *ashram*, I saw a new radio sitting on the stand next to him. This one had more channels, could play cassette tapes and could connect to the large speakers in the meditation hall. A Japanese passerby had gifted the music player to him.

For the *Guru* this was an exciting gift. Now he could play chants and discourses from other spiritual masters to the audience. As I fiddled around with its dials and switches, he commented with a

13

smile, *"what you receive is exponential to what you give. You just need to give it with a pure heart."*

"Give not because you feel bound to give, give for the pure joy of giving." That was an important standard for each resident of the *ashram* to maintain. At each moment of giving, every *Sevak* and resident had to enquire, "What inner state am I giving from?"

Sometimes I would catch myself giving from a state of attachment. I would give because I sought the receiver's appreciation or approval. Other times, I would give from a lower state of fear, guilt or shame. There were times when I gave something because I feared losing love, or someone scolded me for not having done something right, or someone criticized me for being wrong. I have even caught myself giving from a place of arrogance.

"Start observing what you get back when you give from such a lower state," he invited me once when I privately disclosed to him my inner challenge.

For the next few days I observed all my acts of giving. I noticed that sometimes I was able to give from a place of love and selfless service. Other times I gave from fear, guilt or shame. Sometimes I attached no value to my giving. What I learned was that every time I gave from a lower state, what I received back from the receiver – or some other source – was something unfulfilling.

I always saw, one reason why the *Guru* and his *Sevaks* were receiving so much abundance into their lives was because they always gave from a place of inner abundance. The Universe was echoing back their inner abundance with outer abundance, both

THE SEVEN MYSTICAL LAWS OF ABUNDANCE

material and immaterial.

Once a spiritual seeker from some foreign land suggested the idea of turning some of their services into profit.

Smilingly the *Guru* looked at him and replied, "Why would we want to generate a profit when we already have everything we need and more?"

He seemed detached from the rewards of his actions. "I have everything any human wants," he continued smilingly.

*   *   *

By living his life congruent with the laws of abundance, the *Guru* – and his staff – lived a life of sheer abundance.

One day the *Guru* felt that they should have a new shed where the growing numbers of spiritual seekers could be fed with comfort. The day after he spoke of his intention, work began. Out of nowhere came an army of people, some carrying tools and others, barrows. They picked what nature offered them. Bricks, clay, and thatched sheets were delivered by truck. Bullock carts carried rocks found around the village, and by sundown the foundation of the shed was laid. Within a week, the new shed was serving food to the guests.

There was plenty of good health in the *ashram*. I cannot remember ever anyone falling ill or needing medical attention. Young doctors would often come and stay in the *ashram* and spend their time tending to the ill in the village, but I cannot remember them giving health care to anyone in the *ashram*.

And love flowed everywhere. Everyone – including the animals and plants – felt loved. The *Guru* and every other resident engaged with each other with their hearts. *"May every thought, word, and action be an expression of love,"* said one plaque hanging in the meditation hall. Seekers who came and left always carried home a renewed faith in love.

There were people showing up each day from far and wide to tend to the vegetable garden. It always seemed like their garden defied logic. In his garden, vegetables grew even during off-season. Plants were dense with fruits and vegetables all the time. The local farmers came and grew vegetables in the lands of the *ashram* because the yields were much higher there than in their fields.

"I would have a chat with the plants every day," he would say smilingly whenever guests asked him the secret behind the abundance in his garden.

The *ashram* needed a constant supply of flowers for daily prayers. All those flowers would grow in their garden. The children from the local school had adopted the garden, and each day after school the children swarmed the flower garden like a bunch of bees. They would dig the soil, pluck the flowers, and plant the bulbs they found in the wastelands.

It did not matter if, on any given day, there were ten or a hundred guests staying in the *ashram*. There always was enough milk to serve tea to everyone. It seemed like the cows in the *ashram* knew when to produce more milk.

I never felt that money was a constraint for the *Guru* and his staff. A group of university students visited the *ashram* one weekend every month. They all lived together in a hostel in the city. During their free time they would make handicrafts and sell them in their communities, raise money and hand it to the *Guru*.

THE SEVEN MYSTICAL LAWS OF ABUNDANCE

I would see numerous foreigners going into the cities and speak passionately about the *Guru*, the *ashram*, and the daily practice of the residents of the *ashram*. It was a usual sight to see a seeker 'take a break' for a few days, go to the city and return with a few more people.

On one occasion, a young man – I think he was from Germany – left the *ashram* for a few days to visit the city. When he returned he was carrying with him a thick wad of notes, a significant sum of money. He delightfully handed all that money to the *Guru*. We were all curious where so much money came from.

"Where did you get all this money?" Asked the *Guru* curiously.

"I stood at a busy crossroad in the center of the city and entertained people juggling things," he said with a smile. Until the day he left for his homeland, we called him "juggler".

I remember a girl who stayed in the *ashram* for a few weeks, returned to her land, and wrote back saying that she has decided to keep aside 10% of her lifelong earnings to donate to the *ashram*. Until the time I was connected to the *ashram*, her donations arrived every month.

I have many more stories to tell about the channels through which abundance came into their lives. But I will finish with one last story.

I remember, once there was this man who arrived with a backpack and stayed with us for about six weeks. He would always sit quietly in a corner of the meditation hall during the morning and evening *Satsangs*. I would notice him frequently making notes in a small diary. During the *Satsangs*, seldom did he ask questions.

And one day he left.

That is what we were used to in the *ashram*, seekers always came and left.

In the *ashram* we had a custom. Every day at 11am the *Guru* and the staff would sit down together in a circle, and we would address the affairs of the *ashram*. And one of the affairs of the *ashram* was the donation box.

Each day, the *Guru* would open the donation box. It was fascinating what you could find in the donation box. You could find cheques, gold rings, necklaces, diamonds, cash, all kind of currencies from across the globe, sometimes just a simple piece of paper with a 'thank you' note. You would find all kinds of things in the box.

And this is what the *Guru* would do. He would pull out each thing and give it to the staff to take care of. "Ah, beautiful little message! Parvati, stick it on the wall."

"Ok, sort out the currency and cheques and deposit them in the bank. Gold, put them in the locker box."

One day, we were sitting and sorting, and there was a cheque. It was for forty million US Dollars, donated by the quiet man. The *Guru* looked at it for a few seconds then passed the cheque on to a staff and said, "Give it to the village school. They want to build the school."

That was it. It took about 20 seconds for forty million US Dollars to come and go. That was the *Guru*'s relationship with money.

The man who donated the cheque happened to be – I later found out – the founder of one of the world's most popular cafés. But for the *Guru*, none of that made any impact. He was completely detached from wealth. It did not matter to him if he received a lot or received less. I suspect that he was a billionaire in dollar terms. But he would probably wear one or two same outfits throughout his life.

*   *   *

Lest you think that following the seven spiritual laws of abundance is not feasible in the 'real' world, the story of this *Guru* and his *Sevaks* is not an isolated one. I have come across numerous institutions worldwide that experience this level of abundance. They operate in similar ways and experience similar impact.

Any pursuit of abundance is subject to the seven laws of abundance laid out in this book. Each of the next chapters will explore the seven laws.

* * * * * * * *

1. The Law of Exchange

"The Universe operates in giving and receiving"

S. N. Goenka's journey of offering Vipassana meditation to the world began with his migraines[8].

As a young man he became very successful in business in Burma and at the same time began developing severe migraine headaches requiring morphine treatment for pain. There was a real threat that he would become a morphine addict.

So, he had travelled to Europe and Japan in an effort to find a cure. It was then that a friend suggested that he practice Vipassana with a local meditation teacher.

Initially, the meditation teacher refused to accept Goenka into his meditation course. Only if Goenka was willing to practice according to the prescribed technique – with the goal of purifying the mind – was he welcome. Any physical benefits coming out of the practice would be a by-product of the practice.

Goenka agreed.

That course transformed his health...and his life.

Thereafter he knew that his mission in life was to make this form of meditation available to everyone on the planet.

So, his journey as a meditation teacher began.

In 1969, he started by offering his first meditation course in India. But it was not easy. No one knew him. His initial courses where filled only with his parents and a handful of other acquaintances.

---

[8] http://www.vridhamma.org/; http://www.dhamma.org

THE SEVEN MYSTICAL LAWS OF ABUNDANCE

But he persisted. He knew that he needed to simply continue offering what he was gifted to offer. The first course led to another, and another, and so the meditation continued to spread across India.

One of the unique aspects of these Vipassana courses is that they were offered free of any charge for board, lodging or tuition; the expenses were completely met by voluntary donations of people who want to contribute for future courses. Neither Mr. Goenka nor his assistants receive any financial gain from these courses.

Over the next 10 years, Goenka tirelessly gave his time and effort to his courses. He crisscrossed the country to offer Vipassana, often traveling third class in the crowded Indian trains.

The conditions were often rough; he had little money and less support. In those first years, the courses were in temporary facilities—ashrams, churches, schools, pilgrims' rest houses, hostels, sanatoriums, wherever space might be cheaply available. Each site worked but each had its drawbacks, and always there were the tasks of setting up at the start of a course and dismantling the site at the end.

He had no one to help him; instead he himself would assign rooms at the course site, and at meals he might sit with the students or serve the food. Often a tent functioned as the meditation hall. One night during a course, a storm blew down the tent. But early next morning Goenka was on his seat, chanting to encourage the meditators.

But every day he relentlessly focused on giving what gave him great joy in giving. Soon he started offering his courses in English, given the high demand from foreigners and upon the instruction of his teacher.

At the beginning of each day, he would chant; "From every pore flows gratitude, I can never repay this debt. Living the life of Universal Truth, serving suffering people, sharing the happiness of the Universal Truth with all. This is the only repayment I seek."

THE NEW REALITY

"May Vipassana spread to every land around the world. May all come out of suffering and enjoy real happiness, real peace, real harmony," Goenka spoke of his mission when asked.

In 1976, Goenka's mission had taken a great leap forward. The first formal center was opened in Igatpuri in India through donations from many across the globe. A student of Vipassana, a businessman, bought the land. With the help of volunteers, the center came up. Goenka and his wife had no problems staying in the dorms and using the common toilets like everyone else.

His continued efforts in India led to a dramatic growth. A number of Vipassana centers opened, the Vipassana Research Institute was soon established to do further scientific research on Vipassana, and courses started in prisons, schools, and other institutions. Soon foreign students who have practiced with him before began requesting him to conduct courses in their countries.

Thus from 1979 onwards, the technique of Vipassana began to spread westwards. That year Goenka taught two courses in France, followed by one in Canada and two in the U.K. Soon, he visited not only Europe and North America but also Japan, Taiwan, Australia, New Zealand, Sri Lanka, Thailand, and Burma.

To help meet the increased demand for courses, from 1981 Goenka trained and appointed assistant teachers to conduct *courses. Today there are hundreds of assistant teachers conduct approximately 2500 courses every year.*

There are nearly 200 Vipassana centers and hundreds of other non-center courses across ninety countries. Nearly 200,000 people receive the benefit of this powerful technique each year in more than 50 languages. Many more watch Goenka's discourses via satellite broadcasts.

Goenka has been invited to lecture by institutions as diverse as the United Nations General Assembly, the Indian Parliament, Harvard Business Club, the World Economic Forum in Davos, Switzerland, the Smithsonian Institute, Massachusetts Institute of Technology (MIT) and by the Silicon Valley Indian Professionals Association.

*   *   *

In the material perspective, we like to believe that there is Tom, there is Jerome, there is Natalie. We see them as separate individuals coexisting out of a common interest. The *Rishis*, though, do not see people as individuals separate from each other. Instead, they recognize the Universe as one field where everything and everyone is interconnected, and there is a constant flow of energy. This principle is at the core of holistic *Tantra*[9].

In the holistic *Tantra*, we recognize that the entire manifested Universe is created and renewed in the field that exists between the masculine energy and the feminine energy. And this process of creation and renewal continues all the time. When we give, we create and thrive. When we stop giving, we end creation, and we

---

[9] An ancient Indian tradition of practice

slowly perish. In this field there is a constant play of energy. It is flowing back and forth, back and forth, back and forth.

Look at Bill Gates, the founder of Microsoft. God has abundantly given him money and he is doing a good job these days giving it away. And I see wherever he is focused on, especially some activities in India, he is making a significant difference. And I do not want to judge his motive. What matters is that he is giving.

Similarly, the wisdom of humanity is something that I have inherited from my teachers. And this is the thing I love giving most.

> *"If there is not going to be exchange, there is not going to be a Universe"*

Similarly take a few seconds and ask yourself, "what is it that I have abundantly in order to share?"

Find a non-perishable resource[10], something which you possess abundantly and that you can give. It could be care, love, compassion, patience, inspiration, knowledge, empathy, understanding, humor, your life experiences, a prayer or a thought of gratitude. Every thought, word or action is a medium of exchange.

And share those, because exchange is the nature of the Universe. That will maintain the flow.

The moment you disrupt that flow, the Universe collapses. So, if you decide you are not going to give, then there is no receiving

---

[10] More about non-perishable resources in law 7

THE SEVEN MYSTICAL LAWS OF ABUNDANCE

happening.

The moment I make a choice that "I will stop giving", the Universe that I have created around me – whether it is my workplace, or my home, or my friends circle or community – will start to disappear. You will notice that people stop responding back to your text messages or mails. The invitations you sent out for a party were turned down, or nobody turned up at your parties. Whatever Universe there was will start to collapse.

Once you understand that no relationship, no family, no organization or nation can thrive and grow if exchange is absent, you know how much power you have to nurture abundance.

There is something magically unique and abundant that each one of us has to give. Seven billion people, and there is something unique within each one of us. In some cases, what we have to offer is our life experiences.

During one of my recent flights I had a beautiful 5 minutes encounter with a young man who told me how he was giving to his community from some of the "heavy" experiences that he had been through. The wounds that he received from those experiences had given him some lessons, and some wisdom has come out of it. Today he is using that wisdom to coach young leaders.

He was joyously telling me how much he receives in return from his service. It feels to him as if he is the one being served by his clients.

The sign of infinity is a harmonious

"If you give, so shall you receive"

27

never-ending sign. There is no beginning, there is no end. That is the way of the Universe. Its energy flows non-stop back and forth. It is through this exchange of energy that the Universe exists. If there is no exchange of energy, whether it is a microcosm or the macrocosm, it will perish. It will just die.

Water is a microcosm and a metaphor for the Universe. Flowing water finds vitality when it flows. It sparkles and glows when it flows.

Stagnant water, on the other hand, will decompose. It will grow weed. It will start smelling. It will develop an unpleasant odor.

That is how the Universe is. It needs to flow. And it keeps flowing back and forth in every direction. It is through that flow that the Universe fulfills its potential. It is through that flow that the Universe nourishes itself.

This is the first law; that the Universe operates in exchange.

You have great powers to nourish exchange. Just give and receive.

Giving and receiving are two sides of the same coin. They are integral parts of the same contract between you and the Universe. If you give, you are bound to receive.

Yet, giving and receiving are very difficult for many, if not most. That is because we let our free will get in the way of God's will. Let me explain.

Opening up to receiving

Somebody wants to give you something as an acknowledgment of what you did for them, and you go, "please no! This is free. I'm offering this free. Please don't give anything." You are resisting the flow that the Universe is attempting to bring towards you. That is your free will getting in the way of the Universe's will.

Most spiritually awakened people are great givers. But many have so much difficulty receiving. They feel awkward asking. And they feel awkward receiving. In general, this is true for most adults, unlike a little child who will be so happy to receive, exploding in joy.

Your friend or neighbor gives you something nice, and you go, "Ah, that wasn't necessary."

Or, "Oh, you didn't have to do that."

Or, "Why did you do that?"

Or, when your friend gives you something nice you are busy trying to work out in your head when you can reciprocate. If someone gives you a gift you are immediately thinking, "when is her birthday? I have to give her something in return."

Or somebody invites you for dinner. Instantly you are calculating what to bring along as a gift that is comparable to her generosity. Or you are immediately planning when you can invite her over to your place for lunch or dinner. These are all signs of our difficulty in receiving. This is another way our free will interferes with the Universe's will.

There is a big difference between receiving and taking. Receiving involves being open to what the Universe brings to you. With taking, your free will is involved.

Taking is what many of us do in our relationships; taking from everyone and everything that we have around us. Many of us, we are constantly focused on the questions, "what is in it for me?" and, "what could I take out of this relationship?". That is the motive why some people are working or are in a relationship. There is a little limitation with that motive though.

You can only take as much as somebody is willing to give to you. Constantly, consciously or unconsciously, some of us are giving to those people who are obsessed with taking from us. And one day you would say, "you know what, enough!". You stop giving, and then there is nothing for that person to receive. Thereafter, that person goes back to living in inner poverty. That is the problem with taking.

What stops us from receiving?

Sometimes it is our fear. Unlike children, many of us adults experience fear in asking. Or we may fear that if someone gives without reason, they want something from us, or that they have an ulterior motive.

Other times, our inner scarcity holds us back from receiving. We feel the absence of self-love. And when we do not love ourselves, we do not trust others being kind to us. Or we feel unworthy, and we believe we have nothing to give.

My invitation is, do not get stuck in yourself and your fears and inner scarcity. Let go of focusing on self, and freely reach out to each other. Then we can both receive.

Stepping into giving

Yet another way our free will blocks the flow of the Universe is by blocking the natural yearning of the soul to give.

All human beings have got this incredible capacity to give. Giving is in our nature; the nature of our soul. Even the worst people you know, the most selfish human beings, they have this incredible capacity to give. You just need to get them to connect with their soul. I have many many stories like that of people from all walks of life; who have been very ego-centric and selfish, and have later experienced a huge shift in their lives and connected with their souls. If you know people who are giving less and taking more, send out a prayer to them to connect with their soul.

When you give, give for the pure joy of giving

While many spiritually awakened people have difficulty receiving, spiritually un-awakened people have serious issues with giving. They are often obsessed with possessing, with hoarding. It does not matter to them that all their taking might burden their peace and presence of mind, or that their neighbors suffer, or their employees are struggling. If the planet is depleted or not, does not matter to them. Their ideology is, "I am successful when I take more and give less".

This state of never-ending hoarding and consumption are all symptoms of spiritual un-awakedness. Such people are rich in resources and poor in wealth. For all the material opulence they have in their lives, they suffer from severe inner scarcity (more of this in chapter 2).

When you give, give for the pure joy of giving, and not due to a sense of obligation. That is true giving, the kind of giving that nurtures abundance. I have people in my life who are beautiful examples of that. You all know someone like that around you who is able to give for the pure joy of giving. To be able to give like that – for the sheer joy of giving – is a very elevated state of consciousness.

Yet, we come across people who give to others because they feel compelled by fear, guilt or shame.

A few years ago, I was in Durban, South Africa, offering an evening talk. More than a thousand people had assembled for the evening. During the talk, a black lady suddenly burst out crying uncontrollably. So I stopped and gave her a couple of minutes to compose herself. After she had regained composure, I asked, "anything you would like to share?"

She said "I've been giving and giving and giving, and I am exhausted. I am tired of giving. I can't give one bit more."

"Help me understand," I gently prodded her.

"I have two parents, and they keep telling me that I am not being a good daughter." She sobbed as she shared. "So I try to please them by giving even when I don't have."

She continued, "my husband keeps repeating that I am not doing what a good wife does. And I try to give and give and give to him to please him."

After a pause she continued. "And I have two teenage children who keep telling me that if I don't give them what they want, they do not want me in their lives." She looked resigned as she shared.

"So I keep giving, giving, giving. And I am tired. I'm exhausted!" I could sense anger in her voice.

With her children, fear was motivating her to give.

I watch many TV commercials trying to manipulate you by

THE SEVEN MYSTICAL LAWS OF ABUNDANCE

working on your fear.

"Oh, you don't have this washing product for your baby? You are a bad mother!"

"You haven't taken this insurance? What an uncaring father!"

They compel you to make a choice driven by fear. When I give something because I am compelled by fear, it is not true giving. It is the *illusion* of true giving.

The South African lady's husband kept repeating to her that she was not doing what every good wife does. What does a statement like that trigger inside her? Guilt. That is another great way to manipulate people.

"Hey, I sent you a text message 30 minutes ago. I can see on my device that you read the message. For 30 minutes you did not reply." That is my ego punishing you through guilt.

Lastly, the South African lady's parents kept repeating to her that she was not being a good daughter. What happens inside you when you are constantly told, "Oh, you are not a good person. You are not a good friend."? You start believing that you are not good enough. Shame takes you over.

Triggered by fear, guilt and shame, this lady was giving, and giving, and giving. That is not true giving, the type of giving that multiplies abundance. Love and compassion fuels true giving, fear, guilt and shame does not. True giving magnifies the sheer joy of giving.

A young woman I know gives money to her mother every month. She calls it the 'womb fee'. "Every time we meet, my mother keeps reminding me that she carried me in her womb for 9

33

months. She tells me that she nurtured me through my childhood. And she demands that I now repay her," she explained why she calls her payment the 'womb fee'.

She knew that she was not practicing true giving. Her giving was not coming from a place of pure choice. She was not giving from the benevolence of her spirit, instead she was – in her own words – "shamed into giving".

"I feel manipulated into giving even when I do not have enough for myself. And every time I give, it feels to me like the worst act of the day. For the next few days I carry this burden of having failed myself," there were tears in her eyes as she shared.

A year later when we met, she told me that she had made a change in her life. She no longer gives in response to manipulation. She continues to give, but now she gives it forward. She acknowledged to me that she has received from her parents, and she remains grateful for that. Today she expresses her gratitude for everything she has received in her life by giving to an organization that supports little girls living in abusive families.

She was a different person from the one I met a year ago. Her eyes sparkled now as she spoke, and there was joy in her voice. Through her practice of giving-it-forward, she was feeling nourished and abundant within.

There is an important lesson for us from her life. At a holistic level, we all have received from others, and we continue to receive. Some of us have received from our parents or teachers. Yet, true giving is not giving in response to what you have received. True giving is when we give because of the natural yearning of our spirit to share.

THE SEVEN MYSTICAL LAWS OF ABUNDANCE

When you follow that natural yearning, give with your palm facing upwards. It is told in the *Mahabharat*[11] that Karna[12] apparently gave with his palms facing upwards, with his offerings laying on his palms. Doing so, he gave the receiver the upper hand. The receiver could take the offering on his own terms.

When you receive, receive with the innocence and glee of a child

That is giving with humility. The opposite of which is to give from a place of condescension. "I am giving this to you," is the attitude of condescension. I see this happening everywhere around me; with nations and with parents. That does not follow the law of exchange.

Giving with humility also means giving without conditions. "I will give you money only if you spend it as I wish." That is not true giving.

When you practice true giving, you will notice a sudden change in the way you experience life. You will find within an abundance that is limitless. You will experience an abundance of grace, love, and happiness.

True giving sets off a chain reaction. The attitude of the people around you will shift. And the receiving that happens with true giving can be instantly seen and felt.

*　　　*　　　*

When either giving or receiving is disrupted, our lives collapse.

---

[11] An ancient Indian epic
[12] A pious warrior depicted in the epic

We slip into a spiritual crisis; inside we will live in darkness, in a vacuum, with a deep un-fulfilment. We would find ourselves constantly struggling for material abundance, or for money, or for comforts, or for love, or for friendship, or for community, or for good health. Often inner abundance evades us.

Therefore, keep out of the way of the Universe's process. When we keep out of the way, the Universe operates properly; giving, receiving, giving, receiving...like the symbol of infinity.

Live in exchange. We as microcosms of the Universe, our lives express the first law of abundance. When you receive, receive with the innocence and glee of a child. Give for the pure joy of giving. Everything manifests and finds vitality in giving and receiving. Giving and receiving is the way of the Universe.

Lastly, now that you know how the Universe operates, that understanding should not be the motive to give. Do not think, "I am giving from my heart, so one day I am going to receive abundance." This is the terrible curse of knowing too much.

Yet the Universe does not give back in the same order at which you have given. The next six laws will explain that.

*   *   *   *   *   *   *   *

2. The Law of Echo

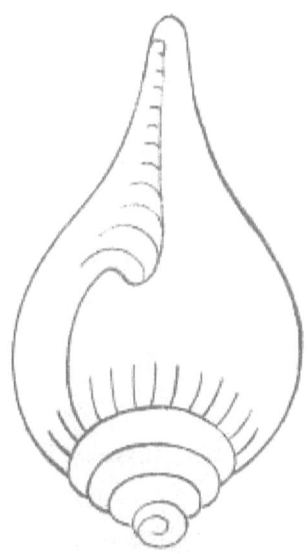

"Everything that manifests around you is an echo of your inner state"

This is a story of a very senior executive lady I once met in India.

"All my staff, all the people around me, everyone who works with me and for me, I give, and I give, and I give to them. However, when I am in a moment of need, I don't receive anything back from them. I ask for help from somebody to do a project, or to create a report, and everybody is suddenly busy. I ask somebody to deliver something, and there is always a reason why it can't be done. When I need help, I ask for it, but it doesn't come. These are all people that I help immensely," she lamented during one of our talks.

I first met this executive at a summit where I was invited to speak to a group of professionals on inner-leadership. We spoke after my talk as I signed a copy of one of my books for her. She was polite and humble.

During our brief chat, I felt like she had a clear idea about what she wanted to chat with me about. She was reflecting on the relationship between heightened inner leadership and effectively leading her team.

The above exchange happened in a later talk.

*"I feel that they are not grateful for everything that I give them."
She was hurting from the lack of reciprocity from people around her. "I am a very generous person. I seldom say no when someone asks me for something."*

She was quite a talented person and had grown rapidly within her organization. As I began to understand her better, it was clear. Indeed, she gave everyday a lot to the people around her.

When I pointed this out to her, she responded, "If someone comes to you for help, isn't that what you would also do?" There was some dismissiveness in her voice. "It is not a big deal."

She grew up in a family where her parents trained her to be generous. "You must give whenever someone asks for help. You must help them," her parents often told her.

She saw generosity practiced at home. Poor people would come and knock on her door, and her parents would give whatever they could; some days food, some days clothes. Even though her parents were not rich, whatever they could afford to give they would give. As a result, this lady, she grew up being generous.

That was the story of this executive.

Somebody would come into her office and ask for something, and she might be busy sending an email, and she would just say "yes" to whatever was being asked. In the process, she would not even look them in the eye.

As she continued reflecting on her patterns together with me, she had a huge revelation. Her heart was not in her giving. She did not attach any value to her giving. In her own awareness, her acts of generosity were nothing.

She gave because she was conditioned that way by her parents when she was a child. She goes on autopilot, gives through the day, and at the end of the day she is exhausted.

"And now when it is my turn to ask for help, nobody wants to help me," she shared in resignation.

*　　　*　　　*

When rewarding you with abundance, the value you attach to your gift and the pure awareness with which you give matters to the Universe.

> *Giving a hug with my full presence is more transformative than anything I give carelessly*

AWARENESS

What I receive is proportional to the level of awareness with which I give something. If I am giving you a book looking you in the eye, with two hands instead of one, I am giving that to you with my full awareness. I am fully present in that giving.

I can give you a hundred thousand Euros with no awareness, or I give you hundred Euros with my heart in it. That hundred Euros is given from a larger space inside me and will be received from a larger space inside you than the hundred thousand Euros that I give off-handedly.

What you give means nothing if your awareness is not in it. You are not going to receive back anything for that hundred thousand Euros. Because the Universe is constantly responding to your awareness of what you give.

The level of awareness with which the executive was giving was very low. What would happen when you give something with such low awareness? When she goes asking for help what does she get?

Say, I am busy texting and you drop by asking for a copy of my book. And I, without taking my eyes off my phone, respond, "of course, you can have one." It does not count as a worthy act of giving in your unconscious. It is of no worth. Because the level of awareness I attach to the act of giving is so low, your unconscious associates no worth to that giving.

In the Dharmic tradition, when we accept holy offerings from the temples or *Rishis*, we accept it with both hands. That represents us receiving it with our wholeness, with our full awareness.

In the Far East, when people exchange business cards, they offer them with both hands. They look you straight in the eye and with a smile on their faces. It is their way of being fully present to the act of giving.

*   *   *

The universe is constantly responding to the value you attach to what you give. Is it not mentioned in the bible that one unit of money given by a poor man is worth a thousand units of money given by a rich man?

You can give a million, and yet receive nothing. Suppose you give a donation of a million dollars. In monetary terms a million might be a significant sum, but are you seeing your donation as an insignificant contribution? If so, the Universe will register your donation as an insignificant contribution as well. Consequently, what comes back to you will also be insignificant.

One of the greatest gifts I love to give to people around me is a carved stick. I would often go into the woods and find a good stick. Then I would mindfully carve it with all my love. Some sticks I would spend days carving, releasing its beauty. Later when I come across someone who has been diagnosed with an illness, or is otherwise going through a tough time, or is having a birthday, or another celebratory occasion, I will gift the stick to that person. The stick costs me very little financially. But there is something else that I give to it; I give it my love, my passion, my thoughts, my well wishes, and my blessings. Though I gift the stick expecting nothing in return, I value that gift as an important gift to give.

*   *   *

Who you are is what you get back

We attract to us everything that we are. Not everything that we ask, not everything we try to possess, but what we are is what we attract. If you are in an inner state of scarcity, it is that scarcity that echoes around. Yet, it is a reality I have complete control over. Because it is my inner state. And through that I have enormous influence and power over everything in my external environment.

Once I find love within, I transcend myself to that state of love. I start noticing love around, it just starts rippling, it starts bouncing back. It starts echoing all around. And I have seen this often in my life when I can step into that state of love no matter what. I start noticing those people who are finding it difficult to share their love with me, they just feel drawn to want to share that love. That is the law of echo.

*   *   *

What I receive is a reflection of my inner state

Here is a little exercise. It is for your eyes only. Take a piece of

THE SEVEN MYSTICAL LAWS OF ABUNDANCE

paper and hold it in the landscape format (for this exercise you would have to use a piece of paper, and not user tablet or other devices). Draw a vertical line in the center. And to the left of the line write down the heading 'Have'. Now take a quiet moment of reflection, and under 'Have' write down one thing you would like to have in your life that you do not have yet. Just one thing please. It could be one thing you would love to manifest in your life that is not manifested yet. It could be anything from a million dollars to just a glass of water.

Having done that, on the right side of the line, write down the heading 'Be/ Live/ Feel.' Now take a few seconds in reflection, then write down in bullets or in short words or phrases the answer to the following three questions;

- ✓ How you would **be** after you received that thing that you wrote down on the left side?
- ✓ How would you **live your life** after you manifested the thing that you just asked for?
- ✓ How would you **feel** inside after you received the thing that you asked on the left side of the paper?

You may have written down "I am grateful", or "I feel happy", or "I'm living my life in ease", or "I'm spending more time with my friends, or "I'm helping others", or "I'm living my passion", or anything else that may have come up.

Once done, drop your pen and study what you have noted on the sheet. 'I want something and when I receive it, I will love my life'. 'I want to become a become a pop star, and once I become one, I am going to be happy and joyful and singing and dancing and relaxing and travelling and be grateful'. Or something else. This is human nature. When we receive something into our lives, we

45

feel fulfilled within. Take a moment to take that in.

Now cut that piece of paper into two along the center line. Place the right piece of paper to the left of the left piece. Take a moment to pause and read the new connections. The 'Be/Live/Feel' now informs the 'Have'.

> *Recognize the plentifulness that is already present in your life*

This is how the Universe operates. When I chose to be happy, to feel grateful, to smile, to laugh, to dance, to sing, to go travelling, or do the thing I love doing, then the thing that I desire for simply comes. The Universe operates exactly opposite to the way our egoistic human condition works.

It echoes back what I carry in my inner state. That is the law of echo.

If I constantly operate from a place of scarcity, all that manifests around me is scarcity. I can choose to feel scarce from within. I can focus on the lacks in my life; say, the love that I miss, the money that I do not have, or the rainy weather. In which case, those lacks will simply continue to perpetuate in my life.

If I operate with fear, all that keeps manifesting are fear factors; there will be a snake showing up, or a guy with a gun showing up.

Like, a child who is walking on the ledge, and the mother screams at him, "oh God! Don't walk on the ledge, you are going to fall." What happens next? He ends up falling the moment he becomes aware of fear.

Alternately, you can choose an inner state of abundance, one of plentifulness. Which is not difficult to cultivate. It involves recognizing the plentifulness that is already present in your life; I have two eyes, two arms, two legs, I have a tongue with which I can speak. If I fall ill, my healthcare is taken care of, I have so many beautiful friends in my life, so many things I can be grateful for. I can smile, I can sing, I can dance, I can laugh. That is all worth celebrating. But we take those things for granted.

Most of us, we live in the world's safest lands. We do not have missiles going around, people randomly shooting us, or us getting mugged. Most of us do not see all of that. We only see the things we do not have.

My inner state is my choice. It is not dependent on the weather, or the number of zeroes in my bank balance, or who I have or do not have in my life. And external abundance just responds. That is the law of echo.

Recently, during one of my inner leadership walks a participant shared his story. "Ten years ago, I was on a wheelchair. I physically could not work. That was when I read the *Artha Shasthra*[13] and other similar books on wealth."

"Soon after, I redefined my relationship to money. I said to myself, 'I am broke, but I am not poor'. Soon, there were a lot of signs telling me, 'I know that you are not moving, but that does not mean you cannot progress.'"

Twenty days later money started pouring in.

*   *   *

---

[13] An ancient Indian treatise on money, statecraft and policy

Practicing Abundance

The root of so many current challenges that people share with me, whether it is hoarding, demanding relationships, controlling and dominating tendency, excessive drinking, compulsive shopping, overeating, perfectionism — come right back to a need to fill the inner scarcity with external opulence. All because we do not feel abundant.

Many of us feel like we must earn our way into abundance. Perhaps I need to have an expensive home, or net a hefty paycheck, or get a lucrative job, or ace in class, or lose 10 kilos, in order to finally feel abundant.

Despite all those material successes, there are many who will never feel abundant. In reality, we do not need to do anything at all. We are abundant just as we are.

We have been measuring 'being abundant' in all the wrong ways. Being abundant is not about what I do or do not do, what I say or do not say, or even who I appear to be.

Being abundant is simple. Each moment I love my life, I am abundant. Each moment I live in the pure joy of giving, I am abundant. Each day that I wake up and follow my heart, I am abundant.

I remember meeting a school teacher several years ago in Canada. I first met him when he was speaking on stage about the future of teaching. He spoke passionately though he was not the smoothest talker.

Later, he expressed to me his dissatisfaction with his speaking skills, a quality, he disclosed later, was important in his 'trade'.

I looked at him and replied, "I watched you on stage. People did not respond to your message because you are a great talker. They liked you because of the genuineness in your life." That struck a chord with him.

"Just be you. Give your gifts. Continue to show that you are real."

The most memorable moment for the audience was when you could not find the phrase you wanted to use. They prompted you, they spoke for you. They rooted for you.

Your power on stage was seen when the audience and you laughed, and then you went on and finished your story.

He has since quit his teaching job and now speaks full time and helps institutions innovate their teaching skills.

Here are some simple practices to keep the energy of inner abundance growing.

1. **Let go of the external and focus on how you really are inside. You are already perfect, lovable and enough just the way you are. So, learn to tune into your being. Allow yourself to feel and listen to those feelings and the thoughts that flow within.**

2. **Practice self-compassion. No matter what, at every given moment, you are trying your best. Any imperfections you carry are imperfections carried by God as well.**

3. **Identify and acknowledge the parts of yourself where you are abundant. Perhaps you have a great talent for**

remembering faces and names. Or, you are able to see the big picture.

4. **Separate your worth from your performance. Your worth is unchanging and is inherent because you were born. Period. Your performance, however, on any given day, in any area may be great or poor. That does not say who you are.**

5. **Recognizing that your being is not tied to your doing. You do not have to prove anything to anyone. You do not have to take control or persuade others to see you in your greatness.**

6. **Practice pureness of intention. May that reflect through every thought, word, or deed. Mean well for others, even when they have not been kind to you. The more you continue with pureness of intention, the more abundance flows your way.**

7. **Trust that the Universe is your ally. Trust that you are already given plenty. Just trusting that whatever next has to come will come. Remember that you do not have to do anything else than being yourself.**

8. **Keep reminding yourself that you are wonder, you are abundant. You are a reflection of the divine. You are Sat Chit Ananda*. You are truth, you are awareness, you are bliss.**

*   *   *

This chapter highlights the reactive part of the Universe. The

Universe is an intelligence that predictably responds to how we show up in life. That is science.

By moving unconsciously through the act of life – having little awareness of the wholeness of people and things around me – I am minimizing their worth. It is that lowered worth that is the basis for the rewards I receive from those people and things. Similarly, if I assign very little value to what I give or the relationships that I hold in my life, what I get back from life will also be diminished in value. That is the law of echo.

What you have around you is just a reflection of what you have inside you. Or, what you do not have around you is a reflection of what you do not have inside you. That is the law of echo.

Because the Universe echoes your inner reality, your inner state determines what you shall receive. If your inner state is one of scarcity, "oh God, I'm miserable, I'm lonely, I'm depressed because I don't have love." What happens? The same loneliness continues to perpetuate in our lives. You will not receive love because the Universe just echoes back your inner state.

My inner state is my choice. It is not dependent on anything that is external to me. When I fully own that choice, I will manifest what I desire. Therefore, I have chosen to own an inner state of gratitude...I have two arms I have two legs, I have two eyes, I have a beautiful family, a great group of friends. I wake up every morning and acknowledge that I can listen to my heart and follow my heart. I am not waiting for money to come before I start travelling. I pack my bags and I travel through four continents every year. That inner state is a choice.

> *My inner state is my choice*

By choosing how I want to show up in my life, I have power over my outer situation. Therefore, by stepping into an inner state of abundance, I am attracting outer abundance as well. For example, when I cultivate self-love within, I will draw love from around me.

* * * * * * * *

3. The Law of Detachment

"What you receive is proportional to your level of detachment from the reward"

I have a great story to share about the law of detachment.

During the mid-nineties I used to know a man from Croatia. He used to work in the shipping industry, and we met during the days when I was a management consultant. He was located in the south of Spain where I was supporting a project for my employers. That gave us the opportunity to spend a few months together.

I liked him very much. He was a happy-go-lucky man, Zen about everything. If his steak was too well-done, he would simply shrug his shoulders and eat it. If the day was washed off, he would go on and settle into a new plan.

This man, he loved football (soccer). Every day, after work we would walk over the nearby community ground where young Spanish kids would play. The Croatian man loved to play with them, and most importantly, he loved coaching those kids.

Most of these young kids – especially the immigrant kids – had no shoes, so they would play football bare feet. He always felt admiration and some sadness for those kids. Every month on payday the Croatian man would buy one pair of shoes for one of the kids. When he received his Christmas allowance, he spent most of it on football gear for the kids.

Since a teenager, every week he used to bet on 'La Quiniela', the lottery on the weekly Spanish football league games. He played it partly for the fun of following the game, and partly to get rich one day. Occasionally he would win the equivalent of a few tens of Euros. When he won, he would go partying heavily. He mostly spent all his wins on women.

Since he started playing with the kids of the nearby community,

THE SEVEN MYSTICAL LAWS OF ABUNDANCE

his motive for betting on 'La Quiniela' changed. He now bet to raise some cash to buy gear for the kids. We were all deeply touched by his commitment to support those kids.

Nothing changed for the first few weeks of betting. An occasional few tens of Euros would trickle in. Those weeks when he would not win anything, he would brood over it and be harsh on himself. Other times, he would seem frustrated and cranky.

Gradually, he started to become obsessed with 'La Quiniela'. He would spend hours studying the teams, their coaches and their players. As the weeks progressed, he became more and more preoccupied with the upcoming games. People around him were getting worried with his attachment to 'La Quiniela'.

Some of his colleagues suspected that he was getting addicted to the lottery. So, they asked me if I would speak to him.

One day I asked him, "how come you are so entangled with the results of 'La Quiniela'?"

He talked about how he really wanted to win big in order to help the kids with whom he played football. "One day I am going to win big in the 'La Quiniela' and use the money to buy football gear for all the kids," he stated fiercely. I was struck by the sincerity of his voice. He really meant it.

An hour into the chat he acknowledged that he was getting too obsessed with 'La Quiniela'.

At the end of our chat, he made a commitment to himself to go back to his old ways of betting on 'La Quiniela'. He agreed to not be attached to the results. He committed to reclaim his playfulness and fun of betting. And that is precisely what he did. Soon, he was back to his old self, jovial, and laughing. When he won nothing, he would shrug his shoulders and say, "last week was fun."

Soon after, we also noticed that he was winning larger prizes from 'La Quiniela'. He was winning the equivalent of a hundred Euros or more sometimes. Though these amounts were very insufficient to support all the kids, we were all pleased for him and the kids.

This continued for months. One day as we were having dinner together, he shared, "I'm glad you showed me the mirror. Thank you for getting me free from 'La Quiniela'.

"Today I'm fully detached from the results of the bets. What we raise from the employees and the bet is not going to fulfill the needs of those kids, but I am happy with how it is. They will keep asking for more, and I will keep offering for as long as I can. It is not sufficient, but I feel at peace with how things are. This is how life is. These kids have needs that I cannot fulfill. But that is how the world is, I guess."

"This is all a game that God plays."

I was struck by his complete detachment from the lottery results. He sounded totally at peace with the imbalance between the needs of the kids and the contributions he could make. He was totally accepting of what is.

I acknowledged him for that and pointed out, "It almost feels like you are now ready to win the big prize."

He just laughed. That evening as we were out for a walk, we walked over to the roadside kiosk and bought a ticket. As we sat down to fill in the ticket, he pulled out his pocket diary to refer to notes about the teams. He wanted to study the recent changes in the teams before filling in his forecast of the results of the *upcoming league games.*

I stopped him. Instead of calculating the outcomes of the weekend games, I asked him to close his eyes and completely detach from winning the lottery. I asked him to stop thinking about getting rich. I urged him to not think about the best teams to win.

Instead, I invited him to think about the kids in the community. I asked him to imagine which teams he would like to see win that weekend. Amused and confident, he crossed the teams according to my request. He was completely detached from whatever the outcome would be.

Three days later he won 1.4 million Euros.

<p style="text-align:center">*   *   ***

In order to understand the law of detachment, it is important to first understand our relationship to money and material possessions.

The most primitive relationship with rewards is the one that corresponds to the survival consciousness. This is the relationship where money controls you. You are thinking, "hey, let us have a pizza tonight." And then you go, "oh, if we go to a restaurant we would have to pay four Euros service charge. Let us take a pizza home instead."

This is the type of relationship where everything – our passion, our love – is being controlled by money or by material possessions. Most people I meet in the East and West alike operate from that state of survival consciousness.

Then there is a big group of people who feel that money does not control their reality, instead they feel that they control money. They feel that money is important for them because it can buy them things they like, but they feel that money does not govern their hearts or control their choices. If their heart calls out to them to become a garden architect, or they wish to own a Gucci bag, they would spend money on them. For them, money is a nice thing to have because it helps fulfill their desires. They see money as a means to an end. That inner state where you are no more controlled by money is a state of transformation consciousness, a state of evolution from the victim self to the free self.

Lastly, there is a category of people who are detached from money. This is a much smaller group compared to the other two. Like children, they are indifferent to the whole idea of money and material possessions. These people are completely led by their hearts and inclined by their passions. They understand their contract with the Universe, that their responsibility is to live their higher purpose. And the Universe in turn assumes the responsibility of providing them with all the resources they need to live their lives. The most elevated human beings among us are in that state of detached consciousness.

This group understands and lives by the law of detachment. As a result, they live an abundant life.

*   *   *

The law of detachment says that the more detached you are from the rewards of your action, the more you receive. How does detachment from the reward look like? In the state of detachment, you are giving for the pure joy of giving. Like when you sit with your friends and play music together. You play for the joy of the music, not expecting anything in return; with

THE SEVEN MYSTICAL LAWS OF ABUNDANCE

complete detachment from the reward.

Therefore, with anything that I am giving, if I can completely relinquish the idea of reward, more and more abundance will flow my way.

My practice of offering all my services on a donation-basis is an experiment in detachment. All the *Rishis* in my tradition, everyone has offered all their God-given gifts on a donation basis (they call it *dana*). This practice has several bases to it.

One important basis of the practice of donation is complete detachment from the rewards of your efforts. This is a deep spiritual practice of liberating oneself from the outcomes.

Several years ago, while considering adopting the practice of offering all my events on donations, I had an encounter with a new age practitioner. There was something about that exchange that struck me.

She had shared with me, "I put a high price tag on the most precious things I have to offer. Otherwise, others will not take them seriously," she shared with me. "If you value your offering, you will put a high price on what you offer too."

Her favourite quote was, "because I care for you and I love you, I put a hefty price tag on what I am offering to you. Because you are paying so much money for my service, you will take it seriously." She emphasized, "you would continue to be committed." She often repeated this to her audience.

Hers is not an isolated example. I have encountered other practitioners who go by the understanding that the more a client pays, the more committed he/she would be to their service.

59

Which is true, for the ego. The ego attaches value to what we receive based on what we have given to acquire it. The ego is constantly measuring what we are worth against what we are receiving. If I am receiving less, the ego concludes that I am worth less.

In order to receive as much as possible – and feel a sense of self-worth – the ego will compel you to give as much as possible, hoping that the other person will reciprocate equally. That is a form of attachment to the rewards.

While I understood the new age practitioner's point of view, it did not resonate with me. So, at my next sitting with my teacher, I brought it up.

"What about making it easy for your clients to choose by putting a price on your service? That can help others determine if your service is something for them," I raised with him.

"How can I put a price tag on the priceless? This wisdom and practices are invaluable for any human being to come out of suffering," was how the teacher responded.

"Besides, when I put a price tag on it, it will match the expectations of some. When I don't, it will match the expectations of all," he elaborated. "Because I do not put a price on my service, everyone can put their own price tag on it," he shared smilingly.

"Practicing the law of detachment means not being attached to the value of what you offer. In the human realm, the value of everything is subjective. A box might mean a lot to you, but to another it might mean nothing," he helpfully explained to me.

"Someone might pay a thousand for your service, another might pay zero. Yet another might pay zero now and give a lifetime of love later. Whatever anyone might pay you depends on what your service is worth to them. Who am I to declare what my service is worth to you? That is for you to determine." I understood his point. I have seen this happen all the time with those I serve. For some, my service is worth the moon, for some it is worth zero. They also donate accordingly.

"When I try to influence the value you attach to my service, it shows that I am attached to the rewards. When I try to put a price tag on my service, it is the same thing. I am trying to persuade you how much my service is worth to you." After a pause he declared, "that goes against the law of detachment."

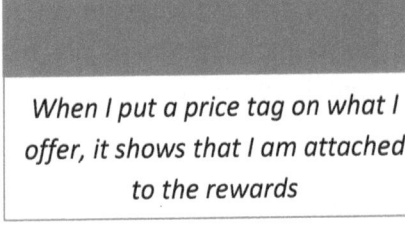

When I put a price tag on what I offer, it shows that I am attached to the rewards

I understood what my teacher was sharing. "Say, you buy yourself a luxury car. You are going to keep it parked in your garage, well-covered. You are probably going to wash it every day. Chances are, you would rarely use it, if ever."

"On the other hand, if you buy an inexpensive, functional car. You will gladly park it by the road side, and you will let bird droppings on it. And you will probably use your garage for storing your family photos rather than take up that space with your inexpensive car.

That is the nature of the ego. The ego attaches value to anything based on the price you paid to acquire it. To the ego, what an item is worth is based on what you have given in order to acquire it.

This is a very important point. You treat something as precious not because it is precious, but because of the amount you paid to acquire it. That is a form of attachment that keeps you obsessed with it, and the universe does not respond to that attachment by offering abundance."

All the *Rishis* and mystics from the *Dharmic* tradition* I have known have lived by the standard that one should not join them for practice – or use their wisdom to change one's life – because you paid a lot of money for it. Instead, join them because you are in the right moment in your life to embrace that path.

In my life, I have tried to adopt that same standard. I try to remain detached from the rewards of my service and welcome you to join my practice not because you paid a hefty sum to join, but because you are at that stage of your life where you are ready for it.

God forbid that you should go through a divorce or have been diagnosed with an illness. Or you have experienced death in your family, or you are having frayed relationship with your children or with your parents, or you are experiencing severe relationship challenges at work.

Then you are committed to your healing and growth. You will jump into my practice with gusto and take full advantage of the power of this work and its wisdom. You are in the right moment in your life to fully embrace the wisdom. You are open to change, you are open to transform. That is the right motive for you to join my practice, and not because you paid a hefty sum.

THE SEVEN MYSTICAL LAWS OF ABUNDANCE

That is my practice of the law of detachment. By remaining detached from the fruits of my labor, I am not influencing how much you value my service. It is not my desire to stimulate your ego and persuade you to come and take advantage of the practice of my tradition. That would go against the practice of detachment.

*   *   *

In Canada and USA, very often I notice posters that say, "Yoga class free!" or "Evening workshop – Free!" And at the bottom the fine print would read, "suggested donation $40".

The moment I say, 'suggested donation $40', what am I signalling to the Universe? My attachment to the rewards. Of course, I would like to use the word 'donation' due to its holy sound. But donation is not donation when there is a 'suggested donation' attached to it. At least not in the sense meant by the Rishis. The practice of offering your services on donation recognizes complete detachment from the receipts. That is what dana[14] implies.

At the same time, I have seen a beautiful practice of the law of detachment emerge in the West; the open source movement[15]. This movement seems to be fueled by the passion of mostly young adults who feel that they are part of a greater whole. Their ability to share ownership of their creation shows detachment from their own creation.

There is an ideological nature to the open source movement, and there is a powerful awareness to it. For those who are new to the

---

[14] Sanskrit word for donation
[15] https://en.wikipedia.org/wiki/Open-source_software_movement

movement, it is centering around the idea that all information should be available to all of humanity, everyone is given the right to use the information, and everyone is free to contribute as they wish.

Too often we get caught up in the dollars and cents of our work and lose sight of the calling that brought us on our path in the first place. In the open source movement, there is an idealism that works to support overall humanity through the work and generosity of its citizens. Those who bear the mantle of contributing to that cause are living examples of those who practice the law of detachment.

I am glad to be part of this movement.

Several years ago, I partnered with a dear friend to start a center to help people fully realize their human potential. We called it BEING AT FULL POTENTIAL[16]. Over the years, we have spent several millions of Euros in research to understand the driver of human potential realization. Everything that we discovered and developed in the center is open source. No copyrights, no trademarks, nothing. We have adopted the law of detachment and put all the intellectual property from the center out there for everyone to use. In return, both my friend and I – and our families – have been blessed with all-round abundance.

Open sourcing what you 'own' is a sign of abundance. If you Google, you will find a growing community of people across the globe who are bypassing the current economic mindset of hoarding and practice the law of detachment. There are numerous examples of communities that uphold new economic systems called the 'gift economy and 'service economy'. These

---

[16] www.beingatfullpotential.com

THE SEVEN MYSTICAL LAWS OF ABUNDANCE

are all living practices of the law of detachment.

*   *   *

As with money, the practice of detachment brings abundance in all our worldly pursuits.

In my spiritual tradition, we recognize that love and joy are meant to be shared, and not to be possessed. A happy, smiling child is a joy to be shared, not possessed. Knowing this, I am aware whenever I meet parents who are very possessive about their child. Some of them would not allow anyone to come close to their child. They impose all kinds of restrictions on their child.

I would notice this behavior sometimes when I would take my little son to the playground. Some parents would marshal their kids out of the sandbox when other kids would sit next to them, or use their toys, or touch them. That kind of behavior is confusing for the child, but for parents who experience scarcity of love, being possessive of their child is a perfectly normal behavior.

The law of detachment says that if you are controlling, possessing or rationing love, it means that you have either experienced loss of love in the past, or you are destined to lose that love that you are trying to possess. Knowing this, my wife and I have made it a practice to share our little son with others. We never shield him from other children or adults who long to share their play or love with him.

If I try to withhold love from others – because I am too attached to love that I do not want to share it with others – that love will one day be taken away from me. Either that, or I have experienced loss of love in the past. It is a beautiful reminder to send out loving kindness whenever I come across people who I see being possessive about their children.

> *If you are possessive of love, it means that you have either experienced loss of love or are destined to lose that love*

A dear friend's brother and his partner recently became parents to a little boy. Since the arrival of the child, they have prevented the grandparents of the child from spending time with him. The grandparents' hearts are filled with much love and kindness, which they are yearning to share with their grandchild.

I do not know the exact reason why the parents have decided to prevent the grandparents from seeing the child. I have heard different theories from different relatives of the couple. Some say that the parents believe that the child is at risk of falling ill due to the presence of others. I have also heard that the parents believe that isolating the child from the others is good for the emotional wellbeing of the child. Apparently, it gives the child the room to bond with the parents.

Whatever the reason, I understand the condition behind the couple's fears. They have either experienced loss of love in the past, or they are destined to lose that love that they are trying to possess. That love that they are trying to possess will be taken away from them by the Universe. That is the law of detachment.

Love is wealth, and wealth is like quicksand. The more you grapple with it, the deeper you get trapped in it. The more you try to grab it, the more it will slip through your fingers. The more you get absorbed with quicksand, the more it will bury you. It will drown you.

The more you obsess over wealth, the less you can have of it. However, the ego naively thinks that it can possess wealth. That goes counter to the law of detachment. I try to possess love, I will always be left without love. I try to possess somebody's life, that person will soon cease to exist in my life.

True wealth is neither a possession, nor a resource. It stems from the Universe. So, detach from it. It will come to you.

*   *   *

Practicing detachment: Having a Billionaire's Heart

Imagine you have a billion Euros in the bank. Someone comes by and asks your help. "I know you love designing websites. Can you design a website for me?" Are you going to think, "you know what, I can charge 500 Euros to do this project?"

What is going to be your motive to design the website?

Your love for designing websites could be the reason why you might design a website for someone, if money is immaterial to you. Putting that love ahead of profit would be practicing detachment from the reward.

Why would I accept your invitation to come over to your land and hold space for one evening? Or offer a weekend practice? Why would I do something if it was not for money?

It would be for the joy of practicing together, or for the passion I have for doing this work, or for the love of the presence of fellow spiritual beings. Definitely not for the reward.

That was an experiment with the law of detachment I undertook a number of years ago. I said to myself, "I am going to follow my calling, but not anymore for the rewards." All my teachers have done it that way. And it felt great for me to follow that tradition.

Yes, there was some fear at the beginning. A part of me was asking, "How am I going to pay my bills? How am I going to buy all the nice things I want in my life?"

Play is love in action

However, there was one guiding question from my teacher that helped me examine my motive each time I said 'yes' to someone who came to me asking for something. "If I were a billionaire and had all the resources in my material life, would I still say yes to this request for help?" If your answer is 'yes', I was practicing the law of detachment. I have a 'billionaire's heart'. I invite you to use this question to develop detachment in your giving.

"How do I find that fine balance between passion and detachment?"

Chanakya – the author of the ancient Indian text *Artha Shasthra*, the text that has significantly informed the seven laws – says that in order to seek success, you must maintain a balanced distance with the source of your success. You must never be too far from it, nor too close.

Like with the case of fire; being too far from it would never let you be able to cook food, but you must also not be too close, as it possesses a threat to your life.

The closeness must be to the effort you put in. Turn your effort into play. After all, play is just love in action. In play, every cell in your body vibrates with the love for your action. Each act fills you up with joy. A student must not study for the sake of getting good

THE SEVEN MYSTICAL LAWS OF ABUNDANCE

grades in the finals, instead she should study for the joy of learning. That is how to become close to the effort.

The distance Chanakya refers to is the distance from the outcomes of your effort. You should never let the result be the motive of your action.

So, find the right distance from the outcome. Check in with yourself. Is the outcome the reason why you are doing something, or are you doing it because you love doing it? When that distance is aligned with the distance the Universe has to that outcome, you become a channel of Its force. Then manifestation moves real fast.

If you are involved in a project, give it space. All projects are just events in the cosmic mind. And these events are vibrating awareness that needs to use their own wisdom and flow in order to fully realize their potential. If you impose your own will over your project or smother it with your attention, its will gets suppressed.

*   *   *

The law of detachment is not only a law of abundance, it is a law that governs all of life. It is also the most misunderstood law.

Why? Because most of us are used to the credo that to achieve something, we must exert ourselves to the maximum. In an action-driven world, the law of detachment feels passive. Plus, there is our ego acting full-force day in and day out, controlling every event in our daily living. We panic when things seem out of order. We lose our cool when things seem out of place. Our insecurities make it difficult for us to let go and observe the law of detachment in our daily lives.

69

Over fifteen years ago, I quit my worldly pursuits and fully stepped into the path of my calling. That involved having faith in the Universe and Its laws of abundance, and detaching from all rewards.

I understood that there was never a transition point when I could say, "now I have enough abundance in my life to quit my material pursuits and fully practice the law of detachment." It does not work that way. Instead, trust that you will be taken care of by the Universe and take a leap of faith. Trust that by practicing the law of detachment you will be in abundance. I have repeated often, "God is my pension plan."

I meet people who say, "I love making music, but I do that in the weekend because during the day I sell shampoo." Or, "my dream is to become a garden architect. I have another 21 years to retire from my paying job. And then I am going to become a garden architect."

God is my pension plan

There is everything we can do to alter that situation. In life, the easiest thing to attempt is to play the lottery every week. But abundance will elude us because we operate from inner scarcity.

Act instead because your heart is so filled with your love that you want to share your love with others. And not because you want rewards for your action. How rapidly you receive the reward will depend on the level of your detachment from the reward.

* * * * * * * *

4. The Law of Exponentiality

"Receiving is exponential to giving."

I gave out a copy of one of my books to someone I met in Texas, USA, and a year and a half later I received an exponential reward from him.

This is how it went. A while ago, one day I received a donation of US$1700 from someone I did not know. So, after tracing that person's contact details, I sent him a 'thank you' note.

He happened to be from Austin, Texas, USA, someone by the name of Edwin (name changed). Two years before he made the donation, I had been to Austin to offer a talk. My publisher had shipped in a box of my books to be made available during the talk. After every event I offer, I sit at a table to sign copies for those who want them. There would also be a donation basket for those who want to make a donation for the books.

After I had sent the 'thank you' note, Edwin replied asking me if we could chat briefly. I agreed. He opened his heart and life to me on that skype call. He told me that he had recently gone through a divorce. His wife had decided to leave him for another man with whom she was having an affair. Edwin was devastated, he was angry and terribly upset and determined on making the divorce as difficult as possible for his wife.

It was then, in a moment of loneliness and anger, that his eyes fell on the book that he had picked up that evening in Austin. On an urge, he pulled out the book and randomly opened a page. His eyes fell upon a paragraph on that page. He read that paragraph, and something shifted within him. He realized in that moment that he was living his life as a victim to a system and the circumstances around him. Lawyers told him what was right for him, and how well he slept depended on his wife's moods and

THE SEVEN MYSTICAL LAWS OF ABUNDANCE

actions.

That evening he realized that he should become the choice-maker of his life. He became aware that he had within him all the resources to be happy. He decided that as of that day he would define his destiny. In that moment, he made a commitment to himself that he was going to go through a compassionate separation.

Thereafter, throughout the whole divorce proceedings he became the champion of his wife's wellbeing. He announced to his wife and to the lawyers that his priority was to ensure that his wife received everything that she asked for.

He shifted his inner reality, and his whole life started to change, including his personal life, work, and financial status. Abundance started to flow in. From being a broke guy, he went on to become financially secure. That is when he decided to donate for the copy that he picked up that evening in Austin.

"I had picked up a copy of the book, but I did not donate anything. I was not in a position to donate anything then. After I decided to make a donation, I went to Amazon (the book store) and found that your book was being sold at US$17. I decided to just add two zeroes to it." Edwin told me over the call. That is how he came to US$1700. Absolutely out of the blue, I had received US$1700.

*   *   **

The story above is a great example of exponentiality. I received exponentially in comparison to what I had given. Edwin received abundantly too. He had found peace when he was struggling with anger. His former wife also received closure due to the support Edwin gave her through the divorce. In all cases, receiving was exponential.

Giving and receiving are not proportional. In the mundane realm of the human mind, we believe that when we give one, we receive one. I give you a loaf

> *Giving and receiving are not proportional*

of bread and you will pay me a dollar. You give me a massage, I give you eighty dollars. That is the wrong understanding of the way of the Universe.

In reality, receiving is exponential to giving. Whether we give good or bad to others, what we receive – or what gets passed forward – is exponential to what was given.

To understand how the law of exponentiality works, it is important to know two sub-laws of abundance.

1.   The Universe Gives Exponentially

From the first law of abundance we already know that the Universe operates in exchange. However, the Universe as we know is also abundant, hence what gets received is exponential to what is given.

Imagine this scenario. Somebody in need asks for a hundred Euros and you decide to give it to her. You are happy to make that contribution. What does that mean for her? The value of that money that she receives is far greater for her than it is for you, or for someone who has no need for a hundred Euros. To her, you have given more than just a hundred Euros. You may have given her freedom, perhaps some peace. Maybe an outlet for her creativity to thrive. The value of what she received is far greater than what you have given. And that is what the Universe counts when it reciprocates your giving.

The same principle counts for pain also. You may have casually traded a few unpleasant words with someone. Or made a general point of criticism on social media against a group. You do not know the measure of pain you may have caused. Someone may have felt offended. You may have brought grief to another. Someone else's sensitivity may have been hurt. All of this is far more than what you may have intended to give. The Universe reflects back to you – a single person – all the pain, grief and hurt you have triggered in countless beings. So, what you receive would be much more than what you give. It would all come back to you sooner or later, in cash or in kind. From the same person who was hurt, or from another.

Many people I know who are active in charity are rewarded exponentially by the Universe in some way or the other. They have pledged their services and money in support of the greater good, and the Universe continues to give back to them tenfold.

Let me share an example from BEING AT FULL POTENTIAL (see previous chapter) on exponentiality.

The mission of BEING AT FULL POTENTIAL is to help people fully realize their human potential. We do that by offering a space for people to step into their true power. That involves taking them out of their self-preservation consciousness, which would automatically get them focused on self-realization. Once we achieve that, people would not anymore be interested solely in making some money to pay their bills. They would start doing the things that they love doing the most. They would begin to truly express their God-given talents.

My friends and I knew that. Hence this movement has been

about helping people identify their God-given gifts and make a choice in life to give or live from that place.

As the project got on, we started noticing some of the people who we were helping, both men and women, started doing incredible things in life. Many have started to follow their dreams, yet others have left their mundane lives in order to follow their calling. One gentleman we have coached has given jobs to 15 other people. A lady we have supported recently released her first book. There are numerous such stories to celebrate.

The project is now a movement. Today across four continents, more than a hundred and twenty distinguished people are championing the movement, while supporting thousands of individuals and institutions make a difference to humanity. And the kind of giving that is happening in the movement is incredible, it is amazing! My contribution has been just that little bit that I have been giving, but what that movement is receiving is a hundred times more today than what I thought I was giving. This is how the law of exponentiality works.

I am sure that you have such stories to tell from your own life. During a recent encounter with a group of three researchers from Canada, I was told that the same law of exponentiality applied to the idea of the Universal Basic Income[17] scheme. If we would offer a small amount to help fulfil the basic needs of the economically underprivileged, what they would offer in return to humanity is immense. Their rewards would be in the form of love, service, financial wealth, gratitude, creativity, jobs, leadership, and more. The Universe being an infinite fountain, it can multiply

---

[17] https://en.wikipedia.org/wiki/Basic_income

what you give and return it manifolds. We will understand more about the infinite nature of the Universe in chapter 7.

2.   To the Universe, Value is Objective

I give you a pen, you receive a pen. Did you receive the same as what I gave? Materially spoken, you could say yes, you received a pen. Holistically though, my act of giving that pen has triggered a chain of more giving and receiving. You, upon receiving a pen, have offered something to someone. It could be a note, or a smile, or something else. That person has also offered something to someone, triggered by your act of giving that pen.

All this could make it seem like it is impossible to measure the value of your giving. That could be true for the limited human mind.

For the Universe though, all value is objective.

Let me explain.

I might not receive the reward of my good deed immediately, it might go to another instead. Hence, I might look at a deal and say, "oh, this was such an unprofitable deal! I invested, I gave, and got nothing back." I might conclude that I received less than what I gave.

In reality, because I gave you something, you had the space in your life to give so much more to somebody else. That is how pay-it-forward[18] works. When you give something, you might receive it back or it will get paid forward. In the end, it will come back to you. In cash or in kind. In thoughts, words or actions.

---

[18] https://en.wikipedia.org/wiki/Pay_it_forward

Suppose Sheila gives one portion of something to Mara. Depending upon Sheila's attachment to her reward, and depending on the awareness with which she gives to Mara, what she gave gets distributed by Mara to others. And one day, Sheila will receive back zero or ten times what she once gave to Mara.

> *When it comes to keeping accounts of your contributions, the Universe is a generous bookkeeper*

This is how value is distributed by the Universe. The Universe will take care of the flow and close the loop. It will pass your gift on to somebody else who deserves it. The Universe is a great book-keeper. And it is also a very generous bookkeeper. It will accumulate the impact your gift had on everyone and return to you accordingly.

Since value is distributed by the Universe, and value depends on each person's needs, to the limited human mind, the value of any object or experience may seem subjective. What is worth highly to you would be worth nothing to another. Hence, what we receive will also seem un-proportional to what we give. That compels the human ego to assign value to things.

By giving a figure to things, your ego can control relationships to its liking. It can set conditions in a relationship. Once you assign a value to something, you know what reward to expect. The ego behaves this way because the complex chain of giving and receiving may seem subjective.

However, the Universe is clear about the holistic value of things. The impact of all the positive and negative things you gave is clear to the Universe. The awareness with which you gave is clear to the Universe. What you gave – whether through a kind deed or a bad act – may have had an impact on many people at different times. This is known to the Universe. As a result, what you receive back from the Universe takes into consideration all that impact. Hence what you receive is exponential to what you give.

It is important to recognize the subjectivity of value to the human mind because there are greater consequences to our actions. What you give ripples 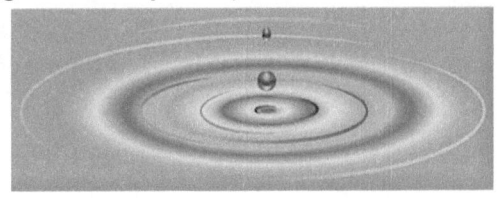 through time and space and touches many. And the Universe gives back accordingly. That makes receiving exponential to giving.

*   *   *

We have great power to attract exponential abundance towards us. We also have the ability to mobilize that power in order to create abundance. That involves understanding how the Universe operates and taking those laws into our lives and practicing. Here are four concrete suggestions that will help you harness the exponential nature of the Universe.

Treat all your actions as sacred

We live in a world where we give to others only to secure tax savings. Relationships are only as good as what it can bring to us. Or when we give, we ask "what is in it for me?" We have turned sacred practices like yoga into lifestyle statements.

Anything sacred we can find, we will drag it down to the mundane. In doing so, we devalue its mysticism and turn it into ordinary.

When we turn something into ordinary, the payoff we receive from it is also ordinary. We have devalued it. So, do not be surprised that what you receive from it would also be insignificant.

I see this happening with relationships these days. We have reduced dating into a mundane practice governed by a set of rules and gambits. Today in many cultures dating is a ritual to be practiced because aloneness is intolerable. As a result, we cannot see each other in our greatness. The other person is only as good as how well he or she can play the game, or what he or she is able to offer me.

The alternative is to hold each other in our greatness. See the other person as a reflection of the divine. Cherish that person's presence in our lives, however short-lived that presence is. And notice how exponentially you receive from them.

Elevate the value of things that you offer and accept. Let all objects acquire the sheen that children see in them. For children, everything is a matter of delight. Everything that they offer or accept has emotions attached to it. When you give something from that place of delight, what you receive also multiplies.

In doing so, we connect to the sacred realm of the Universe, and through that connection we become the Universe. We acquire the infinite potential of the Universe to multiply. We become abundant.

Doing goodness is another HOW

Bring goodness back into all our actions. Your actions towards yourself and others.

Any act of goodness, no matter how small, can have a powerful ripple-effect on others. By goodness I do not mean worship or prayers to Gods, though that could also be part of your goodness. I refer to your daily actions, because practicing goodness is a natural expression of who we are.

Do little things to make a difference and to make others happy. Cheer up someone. It could be the delivery person from a courier or the clerk at the store.

Whether or not they realize it, they will often propagate that same goodness towards others. And before you know it, you have impacted quite a few people. No goodness is menial or unimportant. Anything done with goodness is significant.

Goodness is exponential. The same energy of your goodness is what gets multiplied. It will flood back towards you. There are innumerable opportunities for all of us in a day to give kindness, and if we gave it, imagine the receiving that will happen. Before you know, you are abundant with plenty of what you gave out.

I remember reading once a comment by W. Clement Stone[19] that said, *"Be generous. Give to those you love; give to those who love you, give to the fortunate, give to the unfortunate — yes, give especially to those you don't want to give. You will receive abundance for your giving. The more you give, the more you will have!"*

When you give, give with a full heart

For nearly ten years now I have been supporting a non-profit organization in Europe. This center was founded with the mission of nurturing higher awareness on the planet. It lives its mission

---

[19]https://books.google.de/books?id=OILiBAAAQBAJ&pg=PA54#v=onepage&q&f=false

through offering home to several awakened souls, opening its lands to events and programs on personal growth, living in symbiosis with nature, and in general being a 'lab' for living in higher consciousness.

Since its founding, the center has struggled to stay financially afloat. The burden of its mortgage with a mainstream bank, its conscious choice to be eco-friendly and its spirit of unquestioning hospitality towards its guests has all placed significant financial load on the center. It has continued to pull through due to the largesse of its visitors and workshop leaders, and the labor of its community members.

Yet, from the first day of the center's founding, it has never turned away any person who showed up at its doorstep asking for a place to stay or food to eat. Never has a single person been stopped from attending a workshop due to lack of funds. Frequently, someone who ran away from the harsh realities of his/her work or family life would show up at the center seeking a place to rejuvenate themselves. No questions asked, they are welcomed to spend time in the center. The community members unconditionally uphold the spirit of the center, never expecting anything in return.

Over a year ago, we announced to the world that we would accept donations to pay off the mortgage and free the center from it financial burden. Very soon after, the center received an exponential gift. One of the residents of the community came forward and extended a gift of a hefty sum to the center. He had recently gained a windfall from the growing value of digital currencies and felt called to support the cause of the center.

When I first heard about the financial gift the center received, I was not surprised. I have known the center for nearly ten years, and I have always seen each member of the community give with a full heart. They do not give because they are appraised on it or they expect your acknowledgments, they give for the joy of giving. Each request from a guest is carefully attended to. When someone conducts himself or herself with such pureness and integrity, it is only natural that the Universe responds exponentially.

There is a lesson in this story for all of us. When you give, give with a full heart. Be intentional in your giving. Then others will receive your offer with a full heart. Amazing things begin to happen when you give with a full heart.

What does giving with a full heart mean? It means not computing the value of what you give because you know you will proportionally receive the rewards. That is the difficulty for spiritually awakened people. You know that if you give, you shall receive. Hence, I invite you to ask, "how can I give for the pure joy of giving despite knowing the seven spiritual laws of abundance?"

When you give, give with a full heart

And be fully present when you give something to someone. Acknowledge your act of giving. That could mean not setting up your bank to make automatic transfers every month to some charity that is not vibrating with your soul. That means not sitting behind your PC and making a transfer to a cause. Go out instead and give your offerings with both your hands and your soul. Offer a helping hand to your neighbor.

How present you are in your giving will mean you will receive that much more out of it. The depth of your intention will translate into exponential receiving.

Cherish what you have

I knew a man who was constantly worried about not receiving enough. He would keep tabs on every expenditure he made and every rupee he earned. One day he came to me asking how he could receive exponentially to what he gave.

"I work eight to ten hours each day and put in my best efforts to earn more money," he bemoaned. "I have been working for the same company since 8 long years. But I always seem to have just enough for me and my family. While the juniors under me earn the same amount of money as I do, and I've been giving so much of my expertise to my employer, yet my salary is a pittance. How is it then that the receiving can be exponential?"

He was a very worried man.

"Do you have a house?" I asked.

"Yes, a rather small one." He answered.

"So, you do have a roof over your head. I'm happy to hear that." I acknowledged him.

"Do you have a car?" I asked.

"Yes, I have a new one since last year." There was pride in his voice.

"Do you have a family?" I pried.

"Oh yes!" His face brightened up as he replied. "I have two wonderful daughters who are prolific singers, and my wife and my parents stay with me too."

"God's grace, they are all in good health." He looked

heavenwards as he spoke. "My parents are almost seventy, yet in very good health."

"Does your family love you?" I asked finally.

"Oh yes!" He said emphatically. "Other than a few tiffs now and then, we are a happy family."

After a moment of contemplation, he added jokingly, "it is me who is mostly grumpy around the house."

"You have infinite wealth in your life." I shared my truth with him. "You have a roof over your head, you have food on your table, you and your family are healthy, and you have love in your life. How many people on this planet can claim to have all that you have?"

"You have received exponentially, my friend."

I have grown up learning to cherish what I have in my life. My teachers were those who could pull out the positives in every human being who crossed their path. Every situation is a 'setup' for them, and seldom an 'upset'. That quality of consciousness comes from recognizing that the Universe constantly conspires to provide us with plenty.

This person I met reminds me that I must cherish what I have. Often, we are so busy calculating how much we have given that we are blind to the exponential wealth we have received.

*   *   *

How the Universe operates exponentially is something we need to be aware of in our everyday lives. The Universe is not miserly in giving, and if we just for a day would observe how much we are receiving, it will astound us. Take another day observing how much you gave; in terms of love, care, service, help, kindness, money, hope or a word of inspiration. Have you been giving a lot, or less? Have you made the day for someone you came across this day? Have you been unpleasant or unhelpful towards yourself or towards someone?

Today you may have inspired a friend or a colleague to 'go for it' in life. Or you may have snapped at your child under stress. All that comes back exponentially. Just imagine if we would practice true giving with all the people in our lives. Miracles would happen, and we would actually receive exponentially.

You know that the Universe is exponential. When you give, you are not receiving equivalent to what you give, you are receiving ten times over. Knowing this, the ego can lead you to think that if you give one, you will receive ten. That does not breed exponentially.

If you want to receive exponentially, be fully present while giving, give with a full heart, give for the absolute joy of giving. When we cradle a baby in our arms we may do it with full love. Yet, when we hold the hand of an aged parent we might not do it with love. We might mentally be at ten different places as we converse with our dear ones. None of that is true giving.

Life is too short to be spent calculating what we have received for what we have given. Trust that the Universe will always give back exponentially and be grateful for all you have been blessed with.

*   *   *   *   *   *   *   *

5. The Law of Non-Locality

"Giving and Receiving are Non-local in Time and Space."

At one of my events in Europe, I was addressing a very large group of people. During the break, a lady in her early sixties came up to me and asked, "Sujith, can I catch you for a couple of minutes?"

I welcomed her. She said, "My name is Henriette, and I've been diagnosed with cancer. I've been given between six to eight weeks to die." There were tears in her eyes and her voice broke. "I am going through this process of saying goodbye to my family and friends. It is not easy."

"I am in the middle of closing off all my worldly affairs, and somebody told me about this evening. I felt I wanted to be here." There was conviction in her voice. I thanked her for joining. She went on to say, "I understood from somebody that you have super powers."

She was wondering if there was something that I could do to help her live longer. Without any hesitation I responded, "sure, if you want to live longer, so shall it be." Thereafter, we continued to remain in touch for a few months. She would raise questions about forgiving people, people who she had neglected in the past years, and a former husband who had treated her in a very abusive way.

Step by step, she went through a process of continuing to forgive, and wherever I could help, I continued to. She reengaged with old acquaintances with love, and she brought closure to many things.

She asked me if she could pay me for the support I was offering her. Like I do with all the personal that I offer on this planet, my standard response was, "You know what, I can't respond to that offer because if I say 'yes', I am attached to the reward. It is a reflection you have to go through yourself."

After many months, we lost touch with each other. And about two years later, one day I received an email from a West European legal firm asking me to identify myself. There were some 'matters of significant importance' that they had wanted to settle.

The next time I was in Europe, I made some time to visit them. They studied my identification documents and asked, "Do you remember Henriette?"

I did not recognize the full name. I asked for more information. They said, "you gave her an Indian middle name." I recalled her.

"Well, she passed away a few months ago," the notary informed me. We were having this conversation more than two years after Henriette and I first met during the break of one of my talks. A person who had six weeks to live, lived on for over two years. "She has a letter for you."

In her letter she wrote that the last two years where the happiest of her life. In those years, she had relearned to love, how to forgive and how to see people in their greatness. The beauty in the little things in life, the wonder in all of God's creations was shown to her through her mysticism.

At the end of the note she thanked me for my support in helping her see beauty, and that she has also left the amount of Euros 23,500 for me to use as I wish.

I supported Henriette, and two years later a reward came my way.

*   *   *

It is a very important spiritual practice to recognize that giving and receiving occurs non-locally in time and space. You might extend your help to someone today, and sometime in the future you will receive the rewards of your service from that person or another. Or, in the past you may have already received from someone the reward for this help that you are about to offer today. That is the law of non-locality.

Giving and receiving is non-local in Time

I did feel good that I could help Henriette. For that experience of making a meaningful difference in someone's life, I am available 24/7. It is the thing that gives me the greatest joy. If I get paid for it, good. If I do not get paid for it, good. For my support to Henriette, I got a reward much later in time.

The story of Edwin's donation in the previous chapter is another example of how the law of non-locality in time works. I offered him a copy of one of my books during our encounter in Texas, USA, and two years later I receive a reward.

The Universe operates in non-locality. It is not like in the supermarket; I pick up a bottle of shampoo, and in that very moment I pay. For the Universe, giving and receiving is not a local event. Local in time means, giving and receiving is instantaneous in time. It is here and now that giving and receiving happens.

Since the Universe does not operate locally, and I give something today, then either I may have already received the reward of it in the past, or I shall receive the reward of it in the future.

We live in a world of instant gratification. Instant coffee, instant food, instant cash, instant results...we are rushing through every aspect of our lives. Everything is expected now, and as the pace of the world advances rapidly, we expect results instantaneously. But the Universe follows its own laws. You will be rewarded when the Universe deems it right. Bear in mind that the receiving is bound to happen. So, for everything you give today, you have been given back either in the past or you will receive in the future.

The Universe does follow the notion of time of the human ego. Its abundance is not limited to your current lifetime. In a past lifetime you may have already been rewarded for what you are giving today. The law of non-locality in time spans across lifetimes, and the law stands true across the journey our soul takes. Giving and receiving can happen across lifetimes. You can be rewarded in another lifetime for what you have offered in this lifetime, and vice versa.

You could even call it Karmic balance. You do not know if you are paying something forward or receiving something back. You do not know if the things happening to you now are things that you are paying for a past *karma*[20], or accumulating *karma* to be met with in a future life. These debits and credits are simply the Universe acting non-locally in time.

Giving and receiving is non-local in Space

My story of setting out to offer all my services on a donation basis has been a fear-based one. For years I have been asking myself if I should move all my services to a donation-basis. All the teachers of my spiritual lineage offered all their services on a donation-basis, and I envied their freedom and power of choice. They felt liberated and at ease, being completely free of the strangulating

---

[20] The sum of a person's actions in this and previous lives

worldly bondage of money.

But my fears got the better of me. I worried that people would not donate enough, and I would not have enough. I gave myself excuses.

My first big excuse was that the approach of my teachers would never work for me because my subjects were different. If I tried to share more conventional topics and practices like yoga or meditation, there was a chance that I might raise enough donations.

My second big excuse was that donations worked for my teachers because they stuck to their traditions with discipline. Their traditions gave them recognition. I did not have that advantage.

During my years of doubt, I even used to secretly maintain a spreadsheet. In this spreadsheet I did calculations to see how many clients I would need, and how much and how often would they have to pay for me to make both ends meet. Each time I concluded that no way would I earn enough through the donations of those I served.

When I confided in my teacher of my doubts about offering my services on a donation-basis, he smilingly reminded me, "Karmanye Vadhikaraste, Ma Phaleshu Kathachana"[21]. I still was not convinced.

Then one day I surrendered to the practice of donations in faith. I decided to unshackle myself from my attachment to money and rely on God for the rewards.

---

[21] You have a right to perform your prescribed actions, but you may not be consumed by the fruits of your actions

In the beginning I was tested. I was still attached to rewards due to fear. Once or twice, I almost went back on my intention. Once I even tried mentioning a 'suggested donation' at the bottom of my invitation. Another time I caught myself giving undue attention to a relatively well-off student in the hope of receiving a larger donation.

When I narrated my struggle to my teacher, he firmly stated, "Have faith in the goodness of people and in the 7 laws. Most of all, have faith in yourself."

> *Have faith in the goodness of people and in the seven laws. Most of all, have faith in yourself*

As I continued to master my fears, money started to manifest from the most unexpected sources. Numerous friends who fully believed in my path came forward and extended financial support without any conditions attached to it.

Many extended interest-free loans with no time limits attached to it. So many others stepped forward and offered me their time, some their gifts. Friends help organize my events. Past students would develop websites and create campaigns. Others actively referred my service to their friends. Many would simply just share their companionship and words of encouragement.

One day a friend asked me if I would support a local spa that was struggling to survive. It needed someone with business experience to coach its team and guide them with ideas. My past business experience suddenly came to good use, and their financial reward was well-received.

Around the same time, a local University near where I stayed at that time in Europe asked me if I would coach their faculty. The faculty had expressed a collective interest in bringing their whole selves to their teaching and they felt that I could be of help.

Around the same time, a past student reappeared and offered to share part of her inheritance with me. She had unexpectedly received an inheritance and was looking for a good cause to donate part of it to. She wanted to devote her donation to helping 'awaken the planet', and funding me was her answer. When I heard of her desire, I asked if she would use her donation to organize an events-tour across Europe for me. She did.

I still remember even receiving some unexpected benefits from the local government, something unheard of to my acquaintances. A Cheque from the tax office!

Though what I received as donations from my service was limited, what I received from all sources was abundant. Looking back, I realize it is the Universe's nature to bring abundance to us through multiple channels, not only through the ones that our limited human mind can imagine.

Giving and receiving are non-local in space. That means, just because I give you something does not mean I am going to receive the rewards directly from you. The Universe is conspiring to reward me through you, or through somebody or something else. That is the non-local nature of the Universe in space.

If giving and receiving were local in space, that would imply that when I give you something, the rewards of my action will come from you and only you. Say you get a massage. When you are leaving you pay the massage therapist. You get a service and you pay it right then and there in the same space. Giving and receiving happened here, locally in space. That is not the nature of the

THE SEVEN MYSTICAL LAWS OF ABUNDANCE

Universe. God does not function that way.

Through this book, I am sharing with you what I have abundantly received from the spiritual masters of my lineage. This sharing is happening in this space between us, but what I would receive in return could come from you or someone else. It could be from the tax office in the form of an unexpected cheque. Or it can be from your parents who feel called to give because you are their son or daughter.

Whatever you are giving right now to somebody in your life – it could be your spouse, or child, or employer, or employee - will come back to you through them or somebody else.

I come across coaches and consultants who aggressively review their portfolio of clients and pick out their well-paying clients for special attention. The low-paying clients would be 'weeded out' of their portfolio through disincentives. What these coaches and consultants fail to recognize is that because they are being of service to somebody who really cannot afford to pay a lot, they keep receiving from the paying clients, or from their parents, or receive an unexpected tax benefit from the government.

The abundance coming your way through unforeseen channels is Universe's design for you. Good or bad, you are receiving it because you deserve it. Simply say 'thank you' and accept it. Anything that is coming your way you deserve it. Including if it is coming from your parents.

I know many adults who do not feel comfortable about accepting money from their parents. I have heard them say that accepting money from parents make them feel small. It makes them feel entrapped or limited. Others disclose that they feel embarrassed or ashamed.

99

I have reminded many that if their parents – or someone else – is offering money to them, and if that offer is coming out of the giver's own volition, accept it with gratitude. They are giving to you because of the grandness of their hearts, and resisting their gift disrupts the flow of the Universe.

The message here is, when we give ourselves to what is important to the world – fully and purely – and not just financially, then the receiving comes through many sources. That is the Universe's way of rewarding you for your goodness.

*   *   *

Giving and receiving happens in mundane and unimaginable ways

I first met Rajesh on a TV show where we were discussing the future of the workforce in India. He seemed to be under thirty, and for someone so young, he seems to have done a lot in his life. Since his childhood, Rajesh has been a social activist. He was involved in raising political consciousness among the youth in India, he has worked on employability projects for the underprivileged, and has been involved in empowerment of rural women. His activities were his calling, not his job.

A few years ago, he met with an accident and was bed-ridden for a long two years. He needed money to pay his medical bills that ran into hundreds of thousands of Rupees. Help came from a lot of people, even the watchman of the building he stayed in donated a hundred and twenty Rupees towards his medical treatments. After he got better, he went to find every person who had helped him in his time of need. He was determined to pay them back.

"Many of those who paid for my treatment, I didn't even know them," he told me. "Most of the people who helped me were not expecting to be paid back. So, they were surprised when I showed up with their money."

"It is the most heart-opening experience to meet my donors," he shared. "I often wondered why the watchman would donate, even when he drew a tiny pension each month."

"When I searched out the details of one of the gifters, it turned out that he had passed away." Rajesh recollected. "He was from a poor family, so I felt that his family would be glad to receive the money back. When I went to return his money, his son was there. His son didn't know anything about the donation his dad made. He refused to take the money."

"Since the son refused to take the money his dad donated, I offered to take care of the son's daughters books and uniform until she finishes school." He continues to do that every year.

"It is not in my head that I need to pay back. But I feel this immense sense of gratitude I have for someone who I don't know, who has little income and yet would share his limited wealth to help my treatments." I felt that Rajesh's accident had opened him to the goodness of humanity. He seems to have acquired greater strength to follow his calling.

"Actually, it feels more gratifying to be responsible for the education of his granddaughter." There was pride in his voice. "This is a way of it coming back to the watchman for his kindness."

This story of Rajesh's life is an inspiration for me. It is story of how giving and receiving happens in mundane and unimaginable ways. Rajesh has devoted his adult life in helping the underprivileged, and in his time of need, he received from many different people – some of whom he never knew. A little girl receives books and uniform for what her grandfather had given.

Every day we are subject to the law of non-locality in tiny ways. We are giving to someone at work, or in public transit or in a coffee shop, and we are receiving similar goodness – or bad – from others. Tiny things or experiences are changing hands all the time. Wholeness as a community comes from this daily flow of non-local giving and receiving.

So that is my invitation for you. Stop hoarding your natural spirit and continue to exchange tiny positive things or experiences each day. It could be a smile or holding the door open for someone. You could accept someone's favor or request, if only to make her happy. Doing so, you will enable collective giving and receiving.

The Universe is an infinite non-local entity where receiving happens from the most mundane sources.

Nearly twenty years ago, I used to clean dishes in a student's canteen to pay my way through my master's degree. I did that job for about 20 hours per week for a whole semester. I am so grateful for having had that opportunity to clean dishes, because I knew that this was God's way of paying my bills so that I could continue sharing my abundance with others. I could spend the other eighty hours of the week doing the thing I most loved doing, and that was to help others find their inner leadership and shine in their lives. The pay I received from cleaning dishes was the Universe remunerating me for my service.

I am often reminded that the job that pays our bill is God's remuneration for all the things we give to our family, friends, and community. Often it is through our job that we are rewarded for living our purpose selflessly. Hence, there is little wisdom in condemning our job because it does not pay us what we deserve or does not fill us up with meaning or thrill.

Rewards come often in kind

Often, we associate rewards with money. That is probably the biggest mistake we commit that thwarts the flow of abundance into our lives. Receiving, when happens in kind, is often the best kind of abundance you can ever receive. Keep your hearts open to this receiving, and abundance will flow into your life.

Recently, we were travelling from Puttaparthi, about 200 kilometers north of Bangalore, India, to Kollam in Kerala. As soon

By associating rewards with money, we thwart the flow of abundance into our lives

as my wife and I fixed the dates of our travel, a dear friend invited us. "Hey, please allow me to bring you to Bangalore."

We were to travel by road to Bangalore and from there take the night train to Kollam. Given that we were travelling with our little son and suitcases, we were extremely delighted by his offer and accepted his generosity. He was putting himself out of his way to get us there. We had just received in kind.

Hearing that we were passing through Bangalore, another acquaintance from Bangalore came forward and requested, "Sujith, since you're coming to Bangalore, please start early and spend the day with us. Meet my family. We would very much love to host you for lunch. After lunch, we will drop you at the railway station in time for your train." We went to his house in Bangalore, spent time with his family, talked about our life journeys, and had much laughter and a special lunch meal.

The moment we arrived at the railway station, a young family we know from Bangalore came down to meet us with packed dinner, sweets, and snacks. They came down just to say hello and share their love with us. We met his daughter for the first time and it was beautiful catching up with them, listening to them talk about their dreams, his wife's new career and letting our sons play together for a brief while. This connection with an old friend was receiving in kind.

On board the train, different families in the train were entertaining our son, and he was playing with kids and eating with some of them. Families were generously sharing their toys and food, and keeping him totally entertained. He loved being in the train. There was so much love, laughter, play and fun. These were complete strangers and yet there was so much of connection.

We reached Kollam, and waiting for us at the railway station was somebody dear to us. He simply dropped his work, comes down with a big car, picks us up and drives us forty-five minutes to where we were to stay. The friends with whom we were to stay were not at home as there had been a death in their family. However, they left the home open for us to stay, and their maid was there to welcome us and cook for us. They had thrown open their home for it be our home.

The love and warmth that we experienced from so many generous people during that little trip is receiving of the best kind.

Receiving non-locally in space could mean both materially and

THE SEVEN MYSTICAL LAWS OF ABUNDANCE

immaterially. It could be through matter or energy. Matter could be – among other things – in the form of money, while energy could be – among other things – the experience of love. That is the law of non-locality in action.

When you receive the kind of abundance I shared in the anecdote above, why would you want money or put a price tag on anything in your life? Money cannot buy any of the love and warmth seen expressed by all those people who crossed our path during that short trip.

We could have paid for a comfortable taxi to get to the railway station, or stayed in a nice hotel, but we could not buy this much of love and care as we experienced with those few people along the way. That is what makes this story beautiful.

Receiving happens through different ways, in cash or in kind. The thousand little things we are receiving every day from the Universe, through Its nature, your neighbors, relatives and friends, most people tend to overlook those since they do not count as money. Yet, those are the gifts that make us wealthy.

*   *   *

Our lives are so filled with local transactions in time and space that it is difficult for the limited human mind to grasp the idea of non-locality. How is it possible that I receive a reward from Simone for a service that I offered to Jacob? How is it that I may have already received the reward for a service that I am yet to offer?

However, once you have understood the law of non-locality, giving becomes natural and without any expectation. You trust that the Universe takes care of the accounts commensurate with the service you have offered. You do not expect a reward to come from the same person who you have served.

You know that sooner or later, through us or through others, in cash or in kind, you are served. You know that you do not need anything from others in return for your service, because you may have received in the past or will be rewarded in the future. You have stopped counting what you have received from whom and revel in the abundance that you already have. You do not catch yourself wondering which client is profitable or which relationship is yielding greater benefits. You have become abundant.

You look around and see abundance everywhere. Nature is abundant, it gives without any reservations. Love is abundant, it gives without any expectations. Joy is abundant, the more you spread it, the more you seem to have of it. These are the giving and receiving that are not local to time or space.

> *"If you can give unconditionally, you are a billionaire at heart"*

*   *   *   *   *   *   *   *

6. The Law of Dharma

"The Universe Brings to You All the Resources You Need in Order to Live Your Purpose."

Nearly ten years ago I had an encounter with a young pop singer from California. I first heard her music when she sang some of her songs at a private gathering during one of my visits to her land. Listening to her I knew that she was immensely talented. After she sang, we ran into each other that evening. I asked her if she had any intention to publicly release her music. "Of course, that is my dream!" she said.

Like most young artists, she also was struggling to get her music released. She had done a private recording of some of her best songs and sent them to the big music labels. She received rejection letters from all, but two. One was a renowned label, while the other, smaller one was a niche label.

"That is positive news, isn't it?" I enquired.

"I wish," she answered wistfully. "The truth is, I felt dirty reading the offer from the renowned label. I felt used."

"But I liked the offer I received from the small label." There was more enthusiasm in her voice. "They treated my music with respect. They gave it the acknowledgement that it deserved. However, since they are a non-mainstream label, they need me to finance the recording, launch and distribution."

"Unfortunately, I do not have the money to sign with them." She said with a wry smile. There was sadness in her voice.

"How attached are you to your music?" I asked.

She seemed confused by my question. "It is my music. It is my baby."

"Would you be willing to give away your music?" She seemed

perplexed by my question.

I told her about the age-old custom among the traditional Indian classical musicians of welcoming others to play their music. These musicians see themselves more as conduits of music than as creators. That realization holds them back from claiming ownership of their music. They recognize copyright and trademark restrictions as just actions of the ego. The ego wants to possess what it can and identify with it. The soul on the other hand wants to share, and it rejoices in the joy their music brings to others.

Once I witnessed a music maestro sitting on the front row listening to a group of youngsters play his music. He was mouthing along as they sang, with tears in his eyes. At the end of the show he praised them for playing his music even better than he could.

"I am honored that you have found my music worthy of your lips," was how he acknowledged them.

"Wow, that is beautiful." After a moment of reflection, she added with an innocent smile, "I don't think I am there yet." She meant that she was not ready to dispossess "ownership" of her music yet.

A few days later, I received a message from her. She had decided to put her home-recorded music out in the public welcoming everyone to enjoy it. She uploaded all her music to the internet inviting her friends and acquaintances to enjoy it. She welcomed others to sing it and even change it as they wished.

On her page, she narrated our encounter and the age-old custom among the traditional Indian classical musicians of not assuming control of their art. She also wrote that her greatest joy came not from earning from her music, but from seeing the joy it brought to many.

People appreciated her intent and her gesture. Soon many were enjoying her music widely. Word started to travel about her music and her philosophy behind her music. Several local organizations and communities started to invite her to sing. Local festivals wanted her on stage. She was living her dream of singing for others.

Soon, a group of her friends started to donate small amounts towards her dream. Word started to spread, and to the surprise of the artist, someone started a crowdfunding campaign. Money started to pour in.

About 4 months after we first spoke, she paid the non-mainstream label half a million dollars and signed with them.

*   *   *

The Universe - with all Its abundance - brings to you all the resources you need in order to live your purpose. The money that you need, the love that you yearn for, the good health you desire, the house, the car, the network you want, the friends and the contacts you need, all the resources you need in order to live your purpose, the Universe brings to you. I have seen it happening in my life and in the lives of numerous others I have listened to.

So, what then is *dharma*? *Dharma* could be conceptually defined as the purpose of our existence.

Consciously or unconsciously, we are constantly yearning to fulfill that reason for existence. If you take out all the mundane things out of your life, then all you would want to do every morning when you wake up is to live your *dharma*. Because that is the thing that excites you the most.

Dharma is essentially our deepest longing. It is what fulfills every cell of our body. Once you understand the real essence of *dharma*, you will realize that *dharma* and passion are no different. Passion is just the emotion associated with fulfilling your *dharma*. So, if you do not have any worldly responsibilities or domestic responsibilities, there is a good chance that you will spend the whole day with your passion or with your *dharma*. It is that deepest longing that keeps expressing itself consciously or unconsciously that is our reason for existence. And this longing to realize our *dharma* is the reason why we unconsciously pursue all our material pursuits.

If your *dharma* is to play flute and bring magic into people's lives with your flute, that is it. Play flute. You need not think about any resources. Say your passion is to become a horse whisperer, you think, "how am I going to pay my bills if I become a horse whisperer?"

"My passion is to become a Garden Architect, but hey, my job in the bank is so lucrative. It pays my bills even if it is awful. I hate the bank, I hate my colleagues, I hate my manager, but you know what? My job pays my bills." This is the usual refrain we use to refuse to follow our *dharma*.

Do not hold yourself back from living your *dharma* with questions like, "Will I have enough money? Will I have love in my life? Will I have a house? A car? A network of people?" All resources, the money, the good health, the house, the car you need, it will be given to you. You need to simply choose what your deepest passion in life is. Fully own it, and all the resources you need for you to fulfill your *dharma* - the reason for your existence or your life purpose – will be given to you.

When I came upon my calling, I realized that it was to spread the wisdom of the spiritual masters. I could do it through writing, talks, *Satsangs*, retreats and walks all around the world. But at some point, of time, I recognized that I was not fully realizing my dharma because I was charging for it. My spiritual masters had fulfilled their *dharma* by offering their abundant wisdom to me and not charging a penny for it, and here I was with all the advertising posters for my events with footnote saying, 'suggested donation: $20'.

"Was I completely fulfilling my *dharma*?" I often asked myself. Each time I calculated in my spreadsheet how much I had monetarily received from the event, a feeling of guilt would nag me. Yet we must pay our bills. I had a family and a family has needs.

"How would we survive if I offered all my talks and events completely on a donation basis?" I often wondered. My heart would tug me in that direction. But there was the other part within me that did not completely trust the Universe.

Did that mean that I did not completely believe in the seven laws? Yes. My fears made me question the laws.

After a few years in doubt and tussle with my soul, I finally gave in to my heart and decided to go completely on a donation basis. And guess what the Universe did? It sent my way every resource I needed to fulfill my purpose.

Publishers came forward to publish my books, my friends would finance me in every way they thought possible, there was abundance of love in my life, and my physical health had never been better. I understood from experience that when we really set out to fulfill our *dharma*, the Universe brings to us every resource we need.

"How do you survive if you offer everything you have on a donation basis?", you might ask. I do not keep a score. The thing I know is that the Universe is generous. People are generous. My family and I keep receiving everything we need in order to live a beautiful life.

We do not have a magical income. Yet, every year we travel through four continents, seldom spending money. Whenever we land in a place there are always friends who willingly and joyfully welcome us and take care of our needs. For instance, when we visited Belgium, when my family and I landed there, there was Frank and his partner waiting at the airport. He took me wherever I wanted to go, to do all the things I wanted to do. We slept with dear friends. We all ate and celebrated life together. Friends took us to have the best hot chocolate and waffles. And then he ensured that I was back on the plane.

I could have hired a car and a chauffeur and stayed in a tall hotel building in the city. Instead, we spent our tour with people close to our hearts. We laughed together and shared stories. We went around and visited nice places. We built priceless memories together.

I am living my passion, and the Universe – true to Its promise – brings me all the resources I need to live my purpose.

The Universe brings resources in a myriad of forms

"Do you feel bad when your mom gives you money to do your fun things?" A while ago I asked a young acquaintance of mine who complained about her mother worrying about her.

"Yeah, I prefer earning money on my own and spending it on my own." She replied. "I feel bad taking money from my mom because I don't want to burden her."

"You are not alone," I reassured her. "That is how most people I meet feel."

I reminded her, "Your mother is giving you because her heart is filled with love for you. Who are you to deny that love?"

"You see, I'd rather monetize my gifts than rely on others for their largesse," she shared determinedly. "I wish to fully claim my gift. I love writing, I love being my own boss, I love not getting entangled in a 9-to-5 job.

Before she raised this question with me, she had been through various careers and jobs. Each time she changed jobs, she moved closer to her real gifts. When I first met her, she had just made a switch from a nine-to-five job in the media industry to become a freelancer.

"If writing is your passion, my invitation to you is to continue writing," I encouraged her. "Write whether it is for Times of India, who can pay you, or whether it is for your aunt who wants you to write on her behalf on housekeeping and might not be able to pay you for it."

"Why don't you just consider that you are a billionaire at heart, and from that inner state, why don't you simply start sharing your

THE SEVEN MYSTICAL LAWS OF ABUNDANCE

gifts?"

"Don't worry about the rewards, the rewards will come in multiple ways," I assured her. "And the resources you need in order to continue doing that, whether those resources are money, love, good health, a house, a car, a laptop, or an internet connection, they will come too. If these are the resources you need for you to continue to share your gift with others, then the Universe will bring these resources to you for you to continue sharing your gifts."

Though she was initially reluctant to examine the question I raised, later she did. Consequently, the answers to my invitation created a big breakthrough for her. She began to accept that everything that she was receiving – including those allowances she kept receiving from her mother – was exactly what she deserved. That answer made her fully claim her writing.

Many young people I speak with, when I ask if they are comfortable accepting money from their parents, they give me the same answer. They prefer to be autonomous; they would prefer not to burden their near and dear ones. And I do admire and appreciate that intent of not burdening others.

But if you are receiving something, that is because you deserve it. Whether it is something you receive from your parents, or from your friends, or from your neighbors, or from your employee, it does not matter. There is nothing to be ashamed of or feel bad about it.

Though my family and I live far from our in-laws, every time we meet they slip a little cash into my wife's bag. "Keep it for a rainy day," they say. "Or buy something nice with it." My wife's grandmother still keeps doing the same. This has been going on for years. And there was a time when my wife used to feel bad about that. "You know they are retired. The last thing I want to do is burden them. You know, God is giving us enough from whatever we offer here and there," she used to say. Not anymore. She knows now that if she is receiving, that is because God has decided that she deserves it.

Who are we to go against the will of God? That is your ego playing God. The 'I know it all, I know what is right' idea is you trying to deny the resources that have come your way through the Universe.

"The best you can do is to sport a gratitude-filled heart. That is your reward to those who love you. To those who give to you. Just be able to sincerely say, 'thank you'. And receive with an open heart because you deserve it."

Resources mean just all worldly manifestations, love is a resource, good health, friends network, money, a house, a car is a resource. Our limited mind/ego often associates resource with money. Money is perhaps the worst, but the most commonly expected resource. That is the limitation of the mind that makes it that way. Love as a resource you can actually experience, the house can keep that rain and cold out, money can do nothing of that sort. Money is only as good as what it can buy. If you take a hundred rupee note and give it to a child, it means nothing to him. A child will probably play with it like the way she will play with a piece of paper. It makes no difference to a child. Money is just a means to an end.

The Universe responds to the real underlying resource you need. It does not respond to your prayer from your limited mind. Suppose a little girl wants a new school bag. She might be

THE SEVEN MYSTICAL LAWS OF ABUNDANCE

dreaming of a beautiful new pink school bag.

Since she has learnt from her parents to pray to God for money, she asks God to give her some money. And that is basically the limited mind asking to give her money as a resource. The Universe does not listen to that prayer from her wakeful self. Instead, it listens to her deeper need. The Universe understands this deeper need, and instead of giving money, the Universe may provide a bag, because that is a deeper need. And if you look deeper within, you might discover a deeper need beneath the need for a bag. Perhaps at a deep level, the girl has a need to belong, and she might be thinking that maybe having that bag will make her belong to a group of girls. The Universe will recognize that deeper need, and that need will be addressed.

The Universe responds to the real underlying resource you need

Finding my Purpose

In my late-twenties, wanting to know how to discover my purpose, I visited my teacher. I had just returned from sailing on a ship and was curious to get clear about my greater mission in life. I was living a good life, earning well and travelling to many parts of the globe. But I knew that there was something higher meant for my life. I wanted to uncover it.

"You have been on ships. Have you ever stood on the very front of the ship?" My teacher asked when I requested his help in uncovering my purpose.

These advanced teachers speak in fables and metaphors because they know that nothing registers deeper within your psyche than fables and metaphors. Stories penetrate deep within your awareness and leave the seeds of their wisdom within you.

"Yes," I confirmed.

"When you look out to the front, what did you see?" He enquired.

"Nothing but water," I replied. "All I could see was the horizon and no land."

"Have you ever stood at the very back of the ship?" He asked next. I nodded.

"What did you see?" My answer was the same as before.

I did not have an answer to his next question. "What is different when you look behind versus when you look forward on the ship?"

I noticed no difference between the water in the front or in the back of the ship.

It took me months to figure out the difference in the scenery in the front and back of the ship and understand its significance to my self-enquiry. The difference was the wake, the churn of the water. When you look back into the water behind the ship, you will see miles and miles of the wake in the water. It lies as a straight long line.

In that difference I found the key to uncovering my dharma. The wake represented the trail of all my past; the good and the bad experiences. Maybe you have been a victim of sexual abuse, maybe you separated from a loved one, maybe you were diagnosed with a serious illness, maybe somebody close to you died, maybe a job that you held dearly for years disappeared one *day. All these experiences can be traumatizing. Yet they have conditioned you into who you have become today.*

There are other conditionings that I have been through; the lands I lived in, the values I grew up with, my lifelong journey through mysticism.

I have gone through the experience of connecting the dots of my past experiences. My choice of being born to parents with altered awareness, the early departure of my father, my eventful journey through university, all those past experiences have prepared me for the steps that I am taking today in my life.

That is what the wake meant. It represents all the karma that informs my dharma.

*   *   *

How do I go about finding my purpose? What is my purpose?

We all know the reason why we are born. We were born with that awareness of our reason for existence. Anything that I share with you is not going to help you reach back to that clarity of your purpose. Through a process of addition of more knowledge you can never arrive at your purpose.

To arrive at your purpose, you must undertake subtraction. You must subtract your fear of, "Oh God, how will I survive?"

You must subtract your conditioning, your educational qualifications, your skills, your technical capabilities and most importantly your notions of what is successful. Then what remains will be your awareness of your purpose. You will naturally come to the clarity of what you are born for. Go back into your silence. In that silence you will go back to becoming that new born again. In that place, you will hear what you are designed to live. Become that all-knowing self.

If you simply observe my little son, if he could at this moment put words into his experience, he will tell you why he is born. That is one great way of discovering your *dharma*; watching kids. They express a natural propensity towards their *dharma*. I look at my little son and I can see his *dharma*. This guy is going to become an engineer or a technician. He loves everything technical and mechanical. He loves dancing, music, singing. He loves cooking. He cooks with me. All of this is connected to his *dharma* and he is just two years old. What did you love to do as a child? Maybe your *dharma* is hidden in the pages of your childhood waiting to be opened.

Your *Karma* Informs your *Dharma*

I first met Jodi when I visited a counselling school in North America as a guest teacher. It was my routine to spend two afternoons with the students whenever I was in their land.

Jodi was the quiet type, listening intently and deeply reflective. She hardly spoke, but I could see that she was a serious student.

One of my favorite topics I liked to bring up in class is what the students planned to do after graduation. Most students would talk about their career steps in terms of the market opportunity. In class, they are trained to spot the unserved areas in their market and accordingly position their service. Students would say things like 'there are plenty of women out there who are looking to return to work after having a child," or "there are plenty of those who are looking to re-establish themselves after a divorce".

THE SEVEN MYSTICAL LAWS OF ABUNDANCE

Jodi had a special story. She told us about her years of struggle with drugs, and about her subsequent recovery.

"I have been clean now for five years," she said. "But I carry this constant fear that I might get weak and go back into drugs again. It is not easy. Every day I have to live with this dread. It is always present. I have been lucky to find many different ways to deal with this fear.

"I have been able to create an environment of love around me which helps me stay clean. I have worked on finding deeper meaning and higher purpose in my life that helps me stay engaged in life." She spoke of her gratitude for everyone and everything that came her way.

"There are many others like me out there. They have been through the damaging experience of drug use, have come out of it, and live in constant fear of slipping back. I understand them," there was sincerity and eagerness in her voice.

"I want to help them after my graduation. I want to let them know that they can do it as I have done it. I wish to share with them what I have learned from others before me."

*   *   *

Jodi's *dharma*, she felt, was to help others who have been through a similar experience as she has. I know that to be true because her *dharma* was informed by her *karma*.

"Your *karma* informs your *dharma*" is a beautiful piece of wisdom recognized by the *Rishis*. *Karma*, in the pure sense of the word, is just your life events. All my life events create unique lessons for me to live my purpose – from a past life or this lifetime. The good experiences and the bad ones. All these events bring to us life-

123

lessons; life-lessons that equip us with the ability to fully realize our lives.

That is life's way of preparing you to fulfill your *dharma*. Hence, nothing is a bad event. You can be born to a schizophrenic mother. Just another event. You were bullied in school, just another event. Your dad left you when you were a kid, just another event. You have been sexually abused as a child, another profound event. If you have gone through a painful divorce, that is another powerful event. Somebody dear to you died? Another important lesson. You have been diagnosed with cancer, yet another profound lesson. Even a good experience, born with a loving father or mother is just another event.

You are precisely given all your karma in order to live your dharma

Your *karma* offers you the wisdom and lessons needed for you to fully realize your life. Your *karma* has been given to you to empower you to live your life fully. You simply have to seek into your past events, your *karma*, as you are precisely given all that *karma* in order to live your *dharma*.

In many years of my quest, I have realized what my *dharma* is for this lifetime. I have found the words to express my *dharma* as, **'I'm fully expressing my God-given Human Potential by living my mysticism**.'

That *dharma* is informed by my whole childhood experiences, where I was a non-entity in the lives of my parents. That was painful and dark. However, that was my *karma*, to grow up with a mother who suffered from frequent altered awareness, and a

THE SEVEN MYSTICAL LAWS OF ABUNDANCE

father who was gripped by self-destructive alcoholism.

Because the pain of growing up with such parents was so intolerable that it was a karmic choice to be there, to be born into that life, to be born to them so that I would be informed by that *karma* to choose this path today. That has been an absolute God-given gift for me.

Around me I have seen plenty of misery. And that has done something important for me today. Today I have the simple recognition, "Wow, I am alive!" That life, growing up with my parents, trained me to love every little thing God gives me in life. I have learned to be grateful.

I recognize that I live in an incredibly beautiful country, I have two arms, two legs. I have a tongue to speak with and eyes to see with. There are so many things to be happy about, to be grateful about. These are the lessons my *karma* has given to me.

A man who I met a while ago spoke to me about who he really was, and when I listened to him I felt, "here is a man who is living his dharma." He is very gifted with what he was doing, and that was photography and videography. He definitely has got the skill and talent for that, but there is something else that inspires him that has given him a sense of mission in what he does.

He has a little son that he was not permitted by law to meet. And he missed his son terribly. You could say that was his karma. That was the event he brought unto himself, and because he has experienced that pain, that hurt, that wound, he has made it his mission to bring greater awareness around other fathers' pain of missing their children. It has become his mission. There is a deep connection between his life experience and what he does.

125

That story is an example of your karma informing your dharma.

Among the 7 billion people of the world, you are uniquely blessed with a set of experiences that nobody else has. Your *karma* is yours. Excavate your *karma* and you will know what you are born to accomplish in this moment, both for yourself and for others. It will give you some illumination into your purpose.

Your *dharma* is not informed by your skills, your technical capabilities, your education, or the certificate that you have on your wall, your qualifications. Those are nothing but mere enablers. They are good to have, you know. You are able to do coding, good you have a skill. But it is your *karma* that determines your *dharma*. **You simply need to tap into your life experiences. The more and more you stay with it, the clearer your** *dharma* **will get.**

*   *   *

How often we mistrust and undermine the Universe and Its magnanimity. The Universe is generous and kind, and is constantly waiting to fulfill your deepest longing. But us being the mortals we are, we are not tuned to receiving, and we remain fearful of following our purpose. In fact, I was once asked at one of my events "If your *karma* leads you to your *dharma*, does it mean you're not allowed to make mistakes?"

Our mistakes, our screw-ups are our best lessons. And life is one constant experiment. Sometimes we make mistakes, sometimes not. We are all walking through this journey called life, and we experience many things as we go through it. The mistakes and the wise decisions are all leading us to our *dharma*.

THE SEVEN MYSTICAL LAWS OF ABUNDANCE

Go out and fulfill your *dharma*. You were born to this earth to do exactly that. Do what excites you, fills your soul with joy, and trust that the Universe has your back. It will do everything to make your dreams come true.

*   *   *   *   *   *   *   *

7. The Law of Inexhaustibility

"What is inexhaustible when shared is wealth, what is exhaustible when shared is a resource"

In my mid-twenties I was involved in a business relationship with a friend. Before we launched the business relationship, we had a great friendship where we were sharing love, wisdom, and spiritual practice. Our friendship continued to grow and thrive. We would often meet up and meditate together. He would join some of my spiritual groups.

Occasionally, we would have potluck dinners together with our families and friends. Sometimes we would dine with his parents, on other occasions we would go on picnics or go travelling together with our families. We often celebrated festive days and birthdays together, or occasionally came together with friends.

At some point in our relationship, we had this exciting idea of launching a business together. We felt a common passion for a cause that we wanted to serve.

However, soon after we stepped into business together, all the conversations would be about business and money. Every time we met, we were no more talking to each other about all the beautiful things we used to talk about before. Instead, we would instantly jump into the business aspect of life, exploring it and talking about the strategy and clients. Our quality moments together were spent exploring where to invest what, and how to invest, and who will bear what. All the conversations were around how to nurture the company and build it up.

The most hurting part was that our exchanges were no more about friendship or laughter or wisdom or our spiritual practices. They got all replaced with the new exciting business partnership. Our currency of love got replaced with money.

The business aspects of our lives cannibalized everything else. We were constantly absorbed with the resources related to the business. The transaction of resources took the place of exchange of wealth. The resource part of our lives blocked our sharing of mind and heart. It stole the share of heart we had for the friendship, and after a while our heart connection got replaced with mental engagement around the resource. Towards the end of our relationship, all that we talked about with each other was business and money.

The relationship became formal, transactional, and process-driven. One day, my friend even cooked up a document stating the terms and conditions of our engagement with each other. He believed in the adage that 'a good fence makes a good neighbor'. Our pursuit of resources became so important that we started to stipulate all the 'dos and don'ts' of our relationship. While that was really relevant to a business, that is not congenial to a friendship.

Soon later, a moment of realization came to me. "Oh my God, how our relationship has changed," I wondered. How we were only transacting with each other in resources. We were not transacting at all in wealth. Our relationship had waned down. It was not a friendship anymore.

The only reason why we felt thrilled to really take this business partnership forward was because of our friendship. However, because we stole all the heart and replaced it with our minds, the friendship had completely eroded. All the wealth was replaced with resources.

That foundation of friendship was not there anymore, it was lost. And when it became apparent that it was time to part ways, my friend became quite cold about the whole thing. Eventually, at the end of the story we parted ways. We realized that this was not the way to go.

*   *   *

That experience with my friend in my mid-twenties was my first real life lesson about the difference between wealth and resources. Until then, I was naïve and idealistic about what wealth was.

True Wealth is inexhaustible

During my teen years I have often wondered what wealth is. People around me associated money with wealth. Yet others valued good health as wealth. In Bollywood I heard a song that said, 'I am wealthy because I have love'.

Later in my life I found the answer to what wealth is from the Indian mystics. More importantly perhaps, I learned what is not wealth.

Things that are inexhaustible when shared are wealth. Wealth does not lessen when divided.

Wealth is usually associated with money. However, that is only half true. Money can be wealth in the hands of some and resource in the hands of others. When money is treated in

Unlike resources, wealth does not lessen when divided

accordance with the previous six laws, it becomes wealth. When money is spent as an investment, it is wealth. When you spend money on the upbringing of your children, money can be a wealth. Your children will grow to become further multipliers of money. When money is spent on your own self-realization, money would become wealth. As you evolve, your worth grows.

You bring abundance into the lives of many. When money is spent on the development of the planet and its beings, it becomes wealth. Your spending will help others grow and thrive.

Love is wealth because if you share your love with others, it does not reduce the love inside of you. When you share love, you are not becoming any lesser in love. Your love grows but my love grows as much. Same with joy. I share my joy with you, it does not reduce at my end. It gets multiplied in the act of sharing.

Your passion is wealth because if you are passionate about something and you share that passion with someone, it does not mean your passion will wane. I share my passion with you, your passion arises. You become infused with passion, that does not lessen my passion. It only helps grow my passion.

If I were to say that the Dalai Lama is wealthier than the richest businessman of the world, you would scoff at me. But that is what the truth is. Who would you say is truly wealthy, one with all the things that could perish, or the one with the kind of wealth that is limitless? The Dalai Lama's wisdom and love is the wealth he freely gives away and no matter how much love he gives out, he always has more to give.

Wealth is something that multiplies when shared. It does not reduce when it is shared. A mother loves all her children equally and selflessly. Her time gets divided between them, but - whether she has one child or ten children - her love does not reduce nor gets divided. She loves all her children just as much as she would have loved if she had one kid only. Happiness is wealth. You share your happiness, that makes two people happy, yourself and the other. Your spirit of giving is wealth because when you give, you are happy and the person who receives from you is happy.

Peace, play, service, good nature, hope, and creativity are all inexhaustible. No matter how much you give or share it, you still have it. That is real wealth.

Why is wealth inexhaustible?

Wealth is inexhaustible since it flows from the unmanifest. It comes from a source that has no form. Since the Source has infinite potential, it also has infinite abundance. Anything can be created from it. The Source is a fountain of everything imaginable that can be created.

Love and joy find their origin in that collective Source. Since we are forms of that manifest, our capacity for love and joy is endless. Love and joy are part of our nature. They are part of our design.

The same is true with all wealth. They all find their origin in that Source that is unmanifest. That makes wealth inexhaustible, because the source from where it flows is inexhaustible. There is a limitless abundance as far as wealth is concerned.

Everything that is exhaustible when used is not wealth. They are just resources. While wealth is inexhaustible, resources are not.

The opposite of wealth can be roughly translated as resources. When you share something, if it halves for you, it is not wealth. It is just a resource. Anything that exhausts when you share is just a resource.

Money in the hands of most is just a resource. If I give you half of what I have, then I am only left with half. If I give you all of what I have, I am left with nothing. That means it is exhaustible (unless

THE SEVEN MYSTICAL LAWS OF ABUNDANCE

it is an investment). You spend money, share it, give it, lose it, it gets lesser and lesser. Money is not wealth, not in the bank nor in your hand. All the cars and houses we own, all the possessions we proudly gather are exhaustible, mere shiny objects that can be lost, broken or taken away.

Money, if lessened in the process of giving, is not wealth. But there are situations in life where if I give money to somebody, and my money multiplies with his, then it becomes wealth. In the act of giving money, if you are being filled or you are being enriched, the same money becomes wealth for you.

Let us look at the case of petroleum. If we keep consuming it, it will be finished. That makes it a resource. You cannot say any nation is wealthy of oil, because oil is exhaustible. But you can say that a nation is wealthy of wind. If you harness energy or electricity through wind, it does not mean that the wind will come to an end. In India, sunlight is wealth. If I keep using sunlight, is sunlight going to vanish? No. It is wealth.

Negative emotions like pain and anger are not wealth for they are exhaustible too because when you are in pain and you share that with someone, your pain reduces. You vent out your anger and it reduces.

You have some time in your day, and you decide to spend that time with Christine, you cannot spend that time with Sheila. Because you share it with one, it reduces for the other. That makes time a resource. When you give time to one, you would not have time for another.

Resources are not wealth, you can have a whole lot of it, but they are exhaustible. The more and more we use, the less resource there is left.

135

Why are resources exhaustible? Resources are purely things of the manifested realm. The manifested realm is finite. In this finite realm, things behave in either of two ways.

One, things deplete through use. Petroleum and metals are examples of this. We have limited amounts of both. The more and more we use, the less there is to share. Soon we will run out of it and it will leave us poorer than before. In this realm, we are just consumers.

Two, things get replaced by another. This is the realm of zero sum where when I gain, someone loses. Things only exchange hands. In this realm, we are not multipliers. We are just hoarders.

In either of the above cases, things do not multiply through exchange. Such is the nature of resources.

*   *   *

How we use this knowledge to bring abundance into our lives

If the money I give to somebody is an investment, then it would multiply on every side. But if I spend that money to buy, let us say, a diamond, it stops there. It ceases to be wealth anymore. It becomes just a resource that I used up for myself. But often we use the word wealth carelessly to refer to resources.

A teacher imparts knowledge to 30 students of a class. All of them gain and use that knowledge to further spread the knowledge or use it in their lifetimes. Knowledge then is wealth. Again, next year the teacher will teach another set of 30 students. She does not become any less wise because she has imparted that knowledge once. This cycle of imparting knowledge keeps going on for years and knowledge keeps spreading all through the

THE SEVEN MYSTICAL LAWS OF ABUNDANCE

world. That is unlimited wealth.

The same can be said about leadership. Depending on how it is applied, leadership can be both a wealth or a resource. If it is used to bring out the best in others, you can consider leadership to be wealth. If leadership enhances the lives of people and inspires them to do better, it is wealth.

Yet, some leadership examples we are witnessing around us are divisive and exclusive. Those individuals or institutions are not wealth for most of us since they subtract more from us than add to us. You could call such leadership a resource.

The relationships in our lives, the people we connect with every day, those connections too could either be wealth or resource. When we live our relationships in connection and become fully present to the other, the relationship becomes wealth.

Relationships that are wealth co-create and nurture joy in all our lives. They are not anymore something that exists, simmering somewhere on the back-burner. Instead, they thrive in love and attention. That is the nature of wealth.

Instead, if our relationships keep us small and hold us back from what we are destined to become, they are just resources. They hold us back from fully expressing our God-given potential.

We are choice-makers. In life we have enormous power to attract unlimited wealth into our lives. Other times we can turn resources into wealth. That is a choice that we have.

The first choice that we have is to commit to the consumption and distribution of wealth, and not resources.

If I smile and wish 'Good morning!' to a stranger in the bus, and she does the same to five people in her office, and all those five people speak caringly to even one person they meet, then that single greeting of mine has spread quite a lot of joy. That smile to a stranger is true wealth that keeps growing as it flows. I am no poorer for the want of that smile, and I end up brightening the day for a few random strangers. The chain of smiles keeps spreading. True wealth keeps on growing.

Some individuals and families may seem to have a lot of wealth. But if nobody speaks about them with love, you could consider them to be resource-rich but not wealthy. Wealth for me is, if there is one person who can remember me with fondness and love after I have passed, then I am wealthy. For someone to remember me with love, I may have shared the love that I have with them. Why else would they remember me fondly? That means, I have allowed love to grow. I have shared my wealth. I would rather go for that than the life choices of individuals and families who hold what they have to themselves.

To me it seems like they are very poor despite all the money they possess. Many I know would not want such persons anywhere near them, nor would they want them as role models. All humans have a yearning to feel good about who they are and for the few people they have in their lives. That makes them feel wealthy. So instead of leaving behind resources, leaving behind a sacred legacy would make you wealthy.

The second powerful choice we have is to transform resources into wealth.

For most of us, money is a resource. However, through the conscious use of money, you can turn money from a resource into wealth. Money as a currency is exhaustible, but money as an energy is inexhaustible.

When money is not used as energy, it drains energy from other areas of your life. That is the thing with resources. Resources are zero-sum. When you gain in one area, you lose in another. When you are consumed with the accumulation of resources, you are deprived of time with your family. You will not have time to realize love or to nurture relationships. You would not find time to play.

Today I see the way money being treated, it is purely a resource. The way some people are taking, it is leaving many people worse off. Money in the hands of most people – often the affluent ones – is not wealth because they treat money as a zero-sum game. In their attempt to possess money, they deprive others of it. Sometimes it puts others through slave labor.

The noble work some of the charitable or social organizations do, they turn money into wealth. They are actually giving or investing their money, not possessing. In that process, you are multiplying money. That makes money wealth.

You can do the same. Instead of attempting to hoard, you can make its effect be felt across many. And when you do that, money is suddenly a wealth and no more a resource.

The third choice we have is to become wealthy instead of resource-rich.

That involves taking a different approach to life than is known to many of us.

Wealth is achieved through 'beingness', while resources are achieved through 'doingness'. Let me explain. The conventional wisdom is that to get wealthy, we must work hard. What is wrong with that notion is...firstly, we have misunderstood resource for wealth. If you want to possess resources, you work hard. You belabor yourself, you apply yourself. Whereas attracting wealth is a completely different process. To attract wealth into our lives, we must align ourselves with the Universe.

How we do that? By peeling the layers of our conditioning and refining ourselves until we fully become one with the Universe. The more and more we align ourselves with the Universe, the more and more effortless becomes our capacity to receive and share wealth. The importance of achieving abundance by aligning ourselves with the Universe is critical for our physical and mental wellbeing.

The more you can step into your true being, the more infinitely creative you become. With poetry for instance, the greatest poetry comes to you when you are in that very heightened state of being. Suddenly out of nowhere you feel, "yes! I feel inspired." Words start pouring out. You feel like they are coming from another source that you do not have control over. They are not coming from your head where you are trying to script the words.

This is one real example of how wealth flows when we align ourselves with the Universe. Love, wisdom, caring, inspiration, knowledge, even money flows when we align ourselves more and more with the Universe.

Another powerful choice we have is to live our lives in such a way that we become wealth for others.

Your everyday life can itself be wealth, it is a choice you can make

THE SEVEN MYSTICAL LAWS OF ABUNDANCE

by living true to yourself. And that wealth is shared by truly living a life aligned with the Universe so that you cannot help but inspire others. Mahatma Gandhi and Nelson Mandela[22] are very inspirational world leaders that have shaped the world. The inspiration that flowed from them came from the way they lived their lives. Their lives were completely in alignment with the Universe. They were true to themselves and thus true to the Universe. Their very being emanated the wealth of inspiration.

From the life examples of *Rishis,* we know that the life you live is the lesson you teach.

A large part of my journey has been to release desires. Most people love money because they can spend it on things, many of them resources. I have tried a different experiment. For many years now, I have adopted a standard in my life of consuming less resources and distributing more of my wealth. Every day I ask myself, "what resource can I live without this day?"

My little son has travelled through three continents and has toured over fifteen countries four times already. Every season he is in a different continent, and, like every child, he keeps changing so rapidly each day. Imagine the different types of clothes he needs for different weathers. And the number of toys at all these locations.

One important feature in these years has been that we have not bought a single outfit or toy for him from our pocket. It hurts my wife and I to buy something for him knowing that in two weeks he will grow out of it or becomes disinterested. Thereafter we

---

[22] https://www.amazon.com/Being-Leader-Tracing-Legendary-Leaders/dp/0993721028/ref=sr_1_3?ie=UTF8&qid=1523357496&sr=8-3&keywords=the+being+leader

might consider throwing it away unless we can find another deserving parent who might use them.

Once he liked to have a play kitchen, and then ten days later he was not interested anymore. There are jackets he has refused to wear after the first week. We might have had to throw all that away.

When it comes to possessions and resources, we feel wherever we can give what we have, and wherever we can borrow what somebody is not using, we are content. On three continents, we are blessed to have all the clothes and toys our son needs without buying a single thing. Simply by announcing our relationship to resources to the Universe, and informing our network for what he needs, we have everything. When it comes to clothes and toys, my son is most abundant child on the planet.

Inspired by the way we live – minimal in resources, abundant in blessings from many – countless individuals and families across 3 continents have since changed their lifestyles. Many have overcome their attachment to possessions and reduced their consumption of resources. Numerous others continue to use us as their reference for minimalism. Wherever we go with my events, we become part of the lives of friends who throw open their hearts and their homes for us to stay. We become part of their lives, even if only for a few days. I can gratefully say that we are considered a wealth in some of these people's lives.

*   *   *

Money is a funny thing. Many of us consider it as wealth but do not treat it as wealth. For most of us, money is an egoic pursuit. Money serves the purpose of self-preservation, to help us belong, or reinforce our self-identity.

THE SEVEN MYSTICAL LAWS OF ABUNDANCE

The challenge for us is to turn money into an enabler of our manifested life. Then it becomes wealth like all other wealth in our lives.

Wealth is everywhere. Love, passion, service, ideas, good health, happiness, gratitude, talent, skills, hope, inspiration; they are abundant, they are free. What we choose to do with this unlimited wealth is up to us. The choices that we make can make us wealthy. A slight shift in our mindset can majorly transform your life. Suddenly life becomes easier and happier and immensely abundant.

The understanding that wealth stems from an inexhaustible source can itself change the way we look at money or possessions. The sheen of money can be distracting. It can give you the impression of real worth. Sometimes it can enslave you and make you forget the real wealth that you have in your life.

The power that this wisdom gives us is the choice to use it to see it grow and multiply from money to wealth, a smile to smiles, knowledge to education, kindness to service. The choices are endless.

*   *   *   *   *   *   *   *

SUJITH RAVINDRAN

EPILOGUE

It takes courage to put the seven mystical laws of abundance into practice. I have known some who have panicked and given up midway. However, there is inspiration to be found around us.

If we look around us, the ones who we immediately notice practicing the seven mystical laws are children. Healthy children naturally draw abundance towards them.

Their lives are filled with wealth. Whether in a bus, school or mall, they draw towards themselves infinite love, caring, support. I have always witnessed strangers step forward and shower children with gifts.

How do children attract abundance towards themselves?

They understand the *Law of Exchange*. When their heart is engaged, they give for the pure joy of giving. When they receive, they receive with glee. With children, there is no resistance to give, nor to receive. They do not disrupt the flow of the Universe. They enhance it.

Children live the *Law of Echo* by being filled with infinite possibilities. They are filled with wonder and optimism. For them, everything is possible, until we – adults – tell them otherwise. And that state of inner abundance echoes back into their daily lives.

In the true spirit of the *Law of Detachment*, children are divorced from the outcomes of their actions, and are fully present in the moment. They live in the here and now and turn every moment into play. They are not consumed with the consequences of their actions, instead they are absorbed with what is possible in the present.

Every little thing is a miracle in children's reality. Everything mundane is turned sacred in the hands of children. What they give is furnished with love and fantasy. As a result, what they receive is also magnified compared to what they give. Children are the wizards of the *Law of Exponentiality*.

Children are time-less and space-less. What they received is not considered payback for what they offered. As a result, what they receive is never limited. It just keeps coming and coming for them. Whatever it is that they receive, from whomever it is, they receive as if they deserve it. That is them living the *Law of Non-locality*.

Children fully follow the *Law of Dharma*. Given a choice, every moment of their lives is lived on purpose. They are not driven by any conditioned need to 'have to' do something. That is us adults demanding them to 'have to' do something based on our fears. Leave them alone, and they will simply follow their intuition, and express their natural inclinations.

When it comes to the *Law of Inexhaustibility*, children are alchemists. It is said in the Upanishads, "out of abundance he took abundance, and still abundance remained". Children are multipliers of wealth. They magnify love, their creativity is infinite, they bring play and laughter into the routines of life, and they are able to inspire adults to want to give to them, all by just being themselves.

No wonder then that children are the natural examples of those who draw effortless abundance into their lives. That makes them great teachers for us adults when it comes to the art of attracting

THE SEVEN MYSTICAL LAWS OF ABUNDANCE

effortless abundance towards ourselves.

Children are fully steeped in their 'being-ness'. They are so fully aligned with the Universe that they seem to be channeling the will of the Universe. No wonder then that they attract effortless abundance into their lives, all by just being themselves!

This is the possibility ahead for each one of us. Therefore, keep faith in the goodness of others, faith in your own ability to become all of who you really are, and trust the seven mystical laws of abundance.

I can send you no better prayer.

*   *   *   *   *   *   *   *

www.ingramcontent.com/pod-product-compliance
Lightning Source LLC
Chambersburg PA
CBHW021951160426
4320 9CB000030B/1906/J